The Circle of Life

The Heart's Journey
Through the Seasons

The Circle of Life

Joyce Rupp &
Macrina Wiederkehr

Illustrations by **Mary Southard**

SORIN BOOKS Notre Dame, Indiana

www.sorinbooks.com

ISBN-10 1-893732-82-7   ISBN-13 978-1-893732-82-7

Cover and interior illustrations by Mary Southhard.

Cover and text design by Katherine Robinson Coleman.

Printed and bound in the United States of America.

Library of Congress Cataloging-in-Publication Data

Rupp, Joyce.
  The circle of life : the heart's journey through the seasons / Joyce Rupp, Macrina Wiederkehr.
      p. cm.
  ISBN 1-893732-82-7 (pbk.)
  1. Seasons—Religious aspects—Meditations. I. Wiederkehr, Macrina. II. Title.

BL590.R87 2005
204'.32—dc22

                                                    2004022841

To all the women of wisdom

who have journeyed with us

through our Circle of Life retreats,

and to Mother Earth

who continually enriches us

as we circle through her changing seasons.

Acknowledgments

In the process of writing and publishing this book we have moved through the four seasons a number of times. As we lived through each new season there were always people who enriched our work and became cocreators with us. Heartfelt thanks to:

Rosalie Rueswald, and Wayne and Gayle Vyrostek for valuable affirmations, insights, and suggestions offered to us for improving the book;

Tami and Ron Danielak, Jennifer Sullivan and the Shantivanam staff, Maggie and Bob Wynne for generously providing quiet places of writing for us;

our religious communities—the Benedictines of Fort Smith, Arkansas and the Servites of the American Province—who have been our prayerful companions in the creation of this book;

colleagues and friends who daily make our work a joy: Janet Barnes, Carola Broderick, Paula D'Arcy, Rachel Dietz, Karen Ewan, Ginny Silvestri, Pat Skinner, Magdalen Stanton, and Dorothy Sullivan;

our computer gurus: Pat Bolling, Rick Massingale, Clark McMullen, and Faye Wiliamsen who kept us sane;

Kaye Bernard who believed in *The Circle of Life* and joyfully negotiated our publishing contacts;

Mary Southard for her luminous interpretation of the four seasons;

Rachel Gale, photographer, for making us smile;

publisher Frank Cunningham, editor, Robert Hamma, marketing personnel, Mary Andrews and Julie Cinninger who have all been wonderfully supportive and caring of our work through many seasons;

the memory of our parents: Hilda and Lester, and Marion and Henry who gifted us with the rural living that generated our love for the seasons;

and finally, to you, our readers and participants in our retreats; you are the reason we continue to write.

CONTENTS

SUMMER: SEASON OF FRUITFULNESS 111

 AUTUMN: SEASON OF SURRENDER 163

WINTER: SEASON OF WAITING 225

PREFACE

Every book has a birthing ground,

a moment in time and space

when it is just a bright idea flaming forth

with spontaneity.

Then it becomes a dream resting in

someone's heart and mind

wondering if it will ever see the light of day.

It was autumn in the Rockies. The trail we were on was ablaze with golden aspens. We were enjoying our long awaited free time together and talking about many things. Part of our musing centered around the miracle of our friendship, one that has extended over twenty-five happy years. As we reminisced gratefully, wondering where the future might take us, we paused to observe some exquisite sunlit aspen leaves on a small white branch. Walking on in silence each of us was lost in reverie, enfolded in the quiet beauty of the forest and brilliant azure sky.

Out of the silence our conversation turned to the possibility of writing a book together. We wondered what it might contain. An enthusiastic rise of energy surfaced between us as our creative juices stirred. Out of our dialogue a question emerged, Could we, perhaps, take our passion for life and our growing awareness of the spiritual lessons contained in the four seasons and share this with our readers?

As the warm September sun caressed our skin and the brisk autumn wind blew across our faces, our pondering kept tempo with the stimulating flow of the day's mood. Although we had always lived in two distinct parts of the United States, Macrina in the south and Joyce in the midwest, we both cherished the diversity, challenge, flexibility, mystery, and surprise that we found in each of the four seasons of the year. The thought of writing about these seasons was exciting to both of us.

The two of us had spent most of our lives in ministries involving spiritual growth. We recognized how each of us, as well as those we had companioned and nurtured, experienced these four seasons both internally and externally. Could it be, we wondered, that our book might explore the relationship between the external and internal seasons of our lives? Would we be able to do this in a way that would encourage our readers to reflect on and celebrate these regular turning patterns of Earth and of the human spirit?

This emerging dream was exhilarating but also a bit daunting. We slipped into another contemplative space as we pondered the awesome and challenging task this would mean for us. We were both sisters of the earth. We loved the changing seasons. Exploration of our inner and outer seasons was a natural flow of our journey. Our lives had changed immeasurably because we had discovered a healing spiritual companion in nature. But how could we creatively offer to others a way that would lead them to their own patterns of seasonal growth?

The dream persisted. We imagined offering you, one of our readers, a book you could turn to at any season of the year. If your mood was bleak and your spirit empty, the winter chapter would beckon to you. In those winter pages you would find words that would speak to what you were experiencing. You would learn of the spiritual significance of winter and how all living things need a time of inactivity. You would discover there is a holiness in darkness and a blessing in loneliness that is sometimes revealed only after you have been willing to walk the path without understanding.

Or perhaps it is summertime. You are getting ready to leave for a family reunion when you remember that it's your turn to offer the opening prayer for the gathering. You haven't a clue as to what you will say. Then suddenly you remember this book for all seasons. Such was our dream.

Thus it was in the heart of nature that the book you now hold in your hands was birthed. Writing it has been a rich experience for us. As we entered into spring, summer, autumn, and winter, we tasted each season's flavor, rested in the season's lingering moods, touched with reverence their strengths and blessings, willingly faced their shadows, and humbly accepted their challenges.

We have discovered each season to be a stepping stone in a great circle of life. Round and round they go, no season ever exactly the same as the year before, each one teaching us something more about who we are and about how life is to be lived. We have come to know this circle of life as an ongoing spiral of growth, bringing ever fuller and deeper wisdom into our lived experiences.

It is our hope that *The Circle of Life* will renew your awareness of our planet's seasonal diversity, that it will bring you home to your deepest self where seasonal changes also occur with patterned frequency and graced opportunity. May both the external and internal seasons in the circle of life continue to bless and invite you to greater growth and wholeness.

MACRINA WIEDERKEHR & JOYCE RUPP
SPRING EQUINOX, 2003

INTRODUCTION

Everything the Power of the World does is done in a circle. The sky is round, and I have heard that the earth is round like a ball and so are all the stars. The wind, in its greatest power, whirls. Birds make their nests in circles, for theirs is the same religion as ours. The sun comes forth and goes down again in a circle. The moon does the same, and both are round. Even the seasons always come back to where they were. The life of a human being is a circle from childhood to childhood, and so it is in everything where power moves.

BLACK ELK, TWENTIETH-CENTURY OGLALA SIOUX

The four seasons tell a story of transformation every year. Earth's soil is a graveyard for bones and bark, rocks and feathers, stems and leaves and petals, old logs and grasses, animal skin and fur, foliage and underbrush, and creaturely bodies of all sorts. All these, plus water from the clouds, serve to create a tomb that eventually becomes a womb. Seeds fall and connect with the nutrients of ancient, organic life. Every living thing is a resurrection of something that once died and came to life again, changed and altered by its seasonal journey.

The seasons invite us to honor the earth out of which new life germinates, sprouts, develops, blooms, blossoms, and grows. Listen to Earth's song of the seasons passing through her sacred body. Listen intently to these seasons for they reveal our story of unfolding growth as well. They are reflective of changes in our life. In nature's pages we can read of our own evolving passages from death to life. They repeat themselves over and over as we become more true, more whole, more free with each seasonal turning.

As we enter into the transforming embrace of the seasons we can learn much from the varied moods of their circuitous passage. These moods continually change over periods of time. Summer brings hot temperatures and winter, cold ones. Spring is a vivacious leap into life while autumn is a melancholic lullaby. Each season is one step around the circle of ongoing transformation.

Many images and metaphors describe the pattern of spiritual transformation, but none names it quite so clearly as these four seasons of the physical world. A graceful movement of creative change stirs through spring, summer, autumn, and winter. Here, in the turning of Earth's seasons, the elements of life and death follow one another in a natural, unfolding pattern.

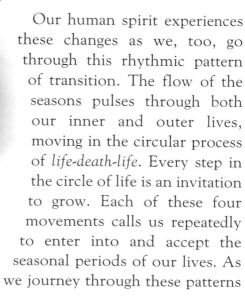

Our human spirit experiences these changes as we, too, go through this rhythmic pattern of transition. The flow of the seasons pulses through both our inner and outer lives, moving in the circular process of *life-death-life*. Every step in the circle of life is an invitation to grow. Each of these four movements calls us repeatedly to enter into and accept the seasonal periods of our lives. As we journey through these patterns of the year and of the heart, each step offers us an opportunity for deeper integration. Each period of change presents us with an opportunity for further development and maturity.

The circle of the four seasons, called "the great round" by the early Celts, is formed by climatic changes as Earth rotates around the sun. Usually these seasons are recognized by a rise or fall in temperature and by the amount of light or darkness that a day holds. Warmer temperatures and the fuller light of spring and summer occur when the rays of the sun shine most directly on the northern or southern hemisphere. The cooler, darker seasons of autumn and winter develop when the sun's rays are at a more oblique angle.

Not all latitudes experience seasons in the same way. Winter may be a harsh, foreboding, frozen landscape in regions close to the poles while in areas nearer the equator it may be continually rainy. Summer offers a welcoming warmth for some places, while others endure many months of extremely humid weather.

In the midst of all these differences, the seasons have one central commonality. They usher in change and growth. Nothing stays the same. It is rare for anything to retain its vibrancy and productivity without some period of dormancy. Blossoms thrive, wither, and fade. Plants grow, then rest awhile. New life arises from seeds that are produced even as the plant dies. As these growing things become compost, they nourish the soil out of which new vegetation emerges. Life and death are partners in the transforming circle of life.

The seasons teach us the art of recycling. Each growing thing rising out of the earth in spring is part of a procession of life that is forever moving through creation. This life is not always visible to the eye. Sometimes life's energy experiences the sacrament of death. Unseen beneath the ground, it rests. However, even in death, life's energy is quietly waiting until it experiences the miracle of some unfathomable breath stirring within, transforming its death into a new creation. That breath circles through our beings, season upon season, offering us the gifts of life and death.

Each season has a unique role to play in this dance of transformation. Spring is the season of resurrection and rebirth. That which was dormant and seemingly dead in winter suddenly wakes up, stretching and leaping with life. Summer develops and matures the growth that began in springtime. It is a season of fruitfulness when the generous gardens and fertile fields fill with ripening produce. Summer does not speak in whispers. It laughs out loud. It is on fire with passion. Summer playfully continues the dance with enthusiasm and vitality.

As the planet tilts away from the sun, the passion of summer begins to weaken and the mellow season of autumn arrives. This is a beautiful period of harvesting summer's gifts. At the same time, a great surrender takes place as the land is stripped of its produce and the hardwood trees lose their leaves. Everywhere change is taking place. Everything prepares for winter. Days get shorter. Darkness lingers. The autumn season is a time of melancholy. A sweet nostalgia is in the air. A homesickness for what seems lost and fading away pervades the earth.

As the rays of sunshine continue to lose their zest, the season of winter emerges, serving as a bridge between autumn and spring. In this season of gestation, Earth waits patiently in silence as she rests from her labors. This inactive period is essential for the land's eventual revival in spring. The furry and feathered creatures as well as the land's vegetation benefit from this fallow time of the year. In this time of seeming death, hidden seeds and hibernating creatures rest safely in the comforting embrace of the earth. The long darkness of winter becomes a nurturing womb.

After the long fallow months of inactivity, the cycle moves into another seasonal mood. Darkness surrenders to light as the days grow longer. Spring comes back like a happy elf, so full of energy it cannot contain itself. It is one continuous emergence of growth, becoming wilder and brighter with each day. Spring entices movement out of every dead thing it lays its eyes on. Life comes tumbling out of winter's tomb, a little wobbly at first, like a newborn calf trying out its legs, but soon it is frolicking with gusto.

Although it may appear that spring/summer, autumn/ winter are opposites, the current of life flows through each season linking one to the other in a balanced, yin-yang relationship. This linking of opposite energies reflects the kinship of one thing flowing into another in a complementary way. Yin slowly changes into yang; then yang into yin. Summer into autumn, autumn into winter, winter into spring, spring into summer. Yang energy is high-spirited and active, always doing more, creating, inventing, celebrating. Spring and summer with their animated, exuberant personalities contain this yang energy while autumn and winter reflect yin energy: inner stillness, contemplation, rest, letting go, being, patient waiting. It is a wondrously holistic evolution that encourages a similar balance in our own lived experience.

Our Inner Seasons

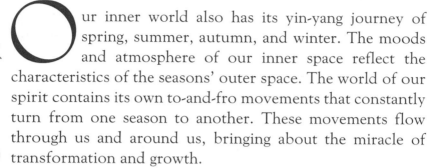

ur inner world also has its yin-yang journey of spring, summer, autumn, and winter. The moods and atmosphere of our inner space reflect the characteristics of the seasons' outer space. The world of our spirit contains its own to-and-fro movements that constantly turn from one season to another. These movements flow through us and around us, bringing about the miracle of transformation and growth.

Who among us has not tasted some of those happy spring-like stirrings when we are full of hope? Our springtime effervescent moods, however, usually move into a more mature and fruitful summertime of creative accomplishments. Although we may be tempted to set up tent in these comfortable places and dwell there permanently, we cannot escape our autumn and winter times. They, too, feed the soul.

Thus, it is reasonable to expect there will be times when joy fades from our lives for a while. We will be ushered into autumn's relinquishment and winter's solitude. Something will be lost so that something new can be gained. Hearing the call to surrender, we will be asked to put on a cloak of trust as we enter into a season of uncertainty. This period of darkness can slip into our lives unannounced. Nothing is predictable or scheduled. Yet, this time of confusion, sadness, and discontent will also pass away. Something bright and hopeful will raise its head over the horizon. There will be another sunrise in our circle of life.

The more we reflect on the seasons of spring, summer, autumn, and winter in relation to our inner seasons the easier it will be to find our personal story hidden in each season's story. The journey of our self is always in one of these seasonal places. The greening spring: vibrant, birthing, life-giving, visioning, delighting, joyful, eager, hopeful, encouraging, laughing. The flaming autumn: nostalgic, reminiscing, dying, transforming, changing, preparing, grieving, gathering, grateful, surrendering, harvesting. The dark winter: silent, waiting, protective, faithful, inactive, nurturing, obedient, sleeping, resting. The bright summer: fruitful, growing, producing, creative, light-filled, ripening, playful, enthusiastic.

These moods live in both the seasons of the earth and the seasons of our heart. Each one is a teacher. Each has its own truth and wisdom, its own challenge and gift. Each beckons us to come further, to live deeper, to find fuller meaning and purpose. Each season can be a mentor and guide for those who live with open hearts.

It is important that we recognize these inner seasons and claim their grace, neither denying their challenge nor being totally dependent on their comfort. It doesn't matter whether we glide, trudge, dance, run, skip, or plod along the way. Our work is to continue to move through these four internal seasons, always willing to receive the valuable teachings they impart.

Our Wise Ancestors

Our early ancestors were more aware of the cycle of the external seasons than we Earth dwellers are today. They gave full attention to the rise and decline of the sun's energy, knowing that the rhythm of the external world greatly affected their life circumstances. They learned to recognize the sun's influence as the cause for the earth's external changes. They saw how life and death were intertwined and how the land responded to light and dark, warmth and cold. They discovered what we now know as the solstices and equinoxes, the precise days when the sun reaches its highest and lowest elevations in the sky and when day and night are approximately equal.

These ancient peoples were so intrigued by this unending pattern that they celebrated each season with energizing rituals of dance and song, just as many indigenous people continue to do today. Their spirits turned with the seasons, allowing their lives to be intricately entwined in these circular patterns of change.

As we enter the mystery of Earth's circle of life, we also enter the mystery of our own circle of life. When we gather to sing and dance on a solstice or an equinox, we are being deliberate about entering into our own seasonal story. When we listen to the rhythms of the planet, we join in gratitude for the mystery and wonder of this constant pattern of growth. With our songs and our dance we acknowledge that we are open to the transforming journey of life.

The four seasons have much to teach us. When we connect our story to Earth's story we gain insight, strength, and courage to live our own evolving and growth-filled journey around the sun. If we listen closely and carefully to the wisdom of each season we will move beautifully and confidently within our magnificent circle of life.

THE FOUR SEASONS

I Arise Today

I arise today with spring in my eyes:

clear circling air

shining inspiration

wings of hope

unfolding buds

happy roots

blossoms of joy

necessary storms.

This is my inheritance in this vibrant new season.

I arise today in the wings of spring.

I arise today with summer in my heart:

fire of enthusiasm

burning sun

abundant life

playful spirit

nesting birds

lush meadows

growing gardens.

This is my inheritance in this vibrant new season.

I arise today in the arms of summer.

I arise today with autumn in my soul:

waters of wisdom

graceful aging

transforming colors

crunching leaves

fruitful harvest

sweet surrender

life-giving death.

This is my inheritance in this vibrant new season.

I arise today in the breath of autumn.

I arise today with winter in my being:

resting earth

gracious darkness

dreaming seeds

barren trees

frosty breath

glowing fireplaces

empty spaces.

This is my inheritance in this vibrant new season.

I arise today in the heart of winter.

MACRINA WIEDERKEHR

The Four Seasons Prayer

···

Sacred Seasons of Earth, as you sweep over our lands and through our hearts, you wear the face of God. How deeply we feel the effects of your many moods. You whisper death chants to us, then lovingly sing out blossoms. You call us into nesting places that we might ponder all that needs to be reborn in our lives. You tell us stories of life and death, transformation and rebirth, stories of waiting, patience, resting, and hope. You enfold us in fruitfulness, then strip us bare. You grow up in us and season us with your temperamental personalities. O Seasons of Earth, bless us with your gracious ability to surrender at the slightest invitation from the Divine Spirit. As you pass over the fields of this earth, open our ears and our eyes that we might discern the wisdom you bequeath to the seasons of our hearts.

WINTER, HUMBLE SERVANT OF CREATION, with brisk determination you encompass our land. You clothe us into warm wraps, sending us out into the weather to gather the lessons you scatter. You call us to sit by the fireplace and feed each other stories. You invite us to listen to that which is invisible. You are the contemplative season. In unseen and unknown places you faithfully do your work. In the winter storms of our lives, teach us patience. May we learn to trust the goodness of what we cannot see. As the ground becomes frozen may we have the courage to visit the frozen ground of our own lives, believing in the life that is hidden. You clear the air. You protect the seed. You embrace reality. You, O Winter, hold our fears until they can be transformed into trust. You are the beautiful season that we sometimes overlook. Share with us your virtues of solitude, contemplation, and faith. Surround us with your fresh, crisp breath and protect the seed that is sleeping in the depths of our being.

SPRING, GRACEFUL, PLAYFUL CHILD OF CREATION, you never walk; you always leap, skip, or dance. You rush in with baskets full of life, giving us all spring fever. We promise to multiply the life you bring by planting new seeds. We will believe in the secret invisible life in each seed as we drop it into the rich soil you have provided. In this season of rebirth, teach us the steps to your dance. Encourage us to celebrate the exuberant life rising around us and within us. Absorb us in the ritual of rising. Remind us never to be ashamed of the beauty that is ours. Bless us, awaken us from productive slumbers that we might believe in the fruit born from the womb of darkness. Your secrets once sleeping in the heart of the earth are stretching toward the sun. Help us to stretch with them as we reach for all we can be. Share with us your virtues of joy, rebirth, and hope. In this season of resurrection, may the brokenness of our world be healed by your contagious spirit and energy.

SUMMER, EARTH'S FRUITFUL SEASON, how rich and fruitful you are. You are the greenest of seasons. Your green is not the pale green of your young sister, spring. It is the bright robe of a forest goddess. From your summer storehouse we receive the oxygen we need each day. Your silent, golden sun greets us each morning and grows more intense as the day wears on. You come to us with arms full of light, long days and short nights. You warm the earth and help the gardens grow that we may be nourished with fruits and vegetables. May we learn from your shining. May we, too, shine on others and lead them to new growth. May we be nourishment for all we meet on the road of life. Teach us to stand still under your green canopy and breathe in the treasures you bring. Invite us to play like a child through your warm, sunny days. You are a sacrament of hope. Your days are full of earth-gifts. Share with us your virtues of passion, generosity, fruitfulness, and faithfulness. May all of these be visible in our garden of life.

 AUTUMN, SEASON OF WISDOM AND TRANSFORMATION, you are the golden season. You come, laughing out a harvest. The ripening of our crops has made the earth a dinner table, and you are the one who serves us. You turn our faces toward the west and remind us of the transitory nature of all things. You call us to surrender. You stir up in our souls a great hunger, a yearning for transcendence. At every moment you are dying to live while we want to live without dying. Teach us the art of surrendering that we might taste the fruit of buried seeds. Teach us to live wisely between our birth and our death. Open our hearts to all that needs transformation. Invite us to join in your beautiful dance of death. Share with us your virtues of acceptance, obedience, and wisdom. Abide with us forever. Transforming, honest season, you know when to let go. Teach us!

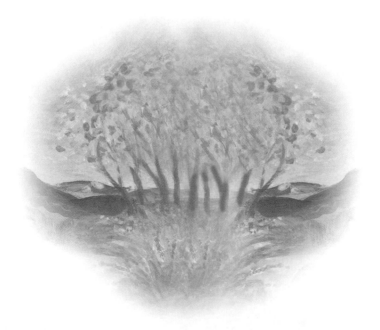

Seasons Speak

Each of the four seasons is a classroom for the heart. If you sink your roots deep into the soil of a season's truth, it can become your mentor. Not everyone lives in a geographical area where the dramatic change of seasons is experienced. Yet the four seasons are a universal archetype for the soul. They are metaphors for the cycles of spiritual growth.

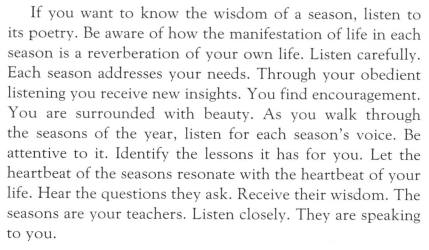

If you want to know the wisdom of a season, listen to its poetry. Be aware of how the manifestation of life in each season is a reverberation of your own life. Listen carefully. Each season addresses your needs. Through your obedient listening you receive new insights. You find encouragement. You are surrounded with beauty. As you walk through the seasons of the year, listen for each season's voice. Be attentive to it. Identify the lessons it has for you. Let the heartbeat of the seasons resonate with the heartbeat of your life. Hear the questions they ask. Receive their wisdom. The seasons are your teachers. Listen closely. They are speaking to you.

Spring Speaks

··

Lean close to the land and touch the soil. Can you hear the pulse of my life in the earth's heart? Can you sense the enthusiasm I have for each new movement of life? In my world, birthing is a daily adventure. Each moment is an invitation to celebrate the experience of new life.

I am the one who awakens the silent seeds from their long winter's sleep. I enter into the glory of each tiny bud as it bursts into bloom. I caress the flowers with gentle breezes. I make them leap and dance with my stormy winds. I take delight in the new green leaves as they begin to decorate the barren trees.

You, too, began as a tiny bud in the womb of your mother. I knew you during the seasons of your formation. I was present at your unfolding. I beheld you as you opened gently to the warming rays of the sun in your life: the sun of kindness and encouragement, the sun of affirmation and love.

Learn to be attentive in this new season of your life, and I will continue to teach you. I want to share my beauty with you now that you are growing older. Beauty is the heart's balm. Each day I anoint you with the beauty and energy of my spring soul. Each day I drink in the joy of being such a lovely season. I know I have the power to lift people's spirits. You, too, have this power. Honor the miracle of your life. Sink your roots deeper into your inner garden and grow strong with healing power. Discover the good medicine of your being. Cherish your potential to be a healing presence in people's lives.

Turn your face toward the streaming rays of life and light. Stand with new amazement at the beginning of every day. Believe in resurrection. Receive life in all its fullness. Leap out of winter's tomb joyfully. Remember that all of your tombs are actually wombs. The seeds of my growth develop gradually in the womb of winter. So do yours. A rich abiding life always lingers near, desiring you to embrace it and claim it as your own. You, too, have the potential to burst forth with new green leaves. Resurrection is your inheritance. Receive it with a song of joy.

Here are a few spring questions for your growing moments. These questions need pondering as much as they need answering.

- What are your memories of lifting the spirits of others by being faithful to the power of spring in your life?

- Who or what was the source of your own spring-power?

- Where in your life are you experiencing rebirth and renewal?

- What is blossoming in you?

- Where do you feel the greatest need for new blossoms?

- What has been your most recent resurrection experience?

- If you were to choose a passage from the scriptures that speaks to you of spring, what would it be?

Summer Speaks

Here I am surrounded by trees filled with fruit, gardens filling up with ripening vegetables, flower beds in the prime of their life. This is my gift to those who embrace my warm, nurturing breath. I observe people basking in the radiant sunshine. They are enjoying the leisurely mood I have provided for them. As I become aware of their summer playfulness, I am content. I glory in the quality of life that has emerged from the abundance of my sun-saturated season. I have a passion for growth.

It has been a joy to watch you grow, also. From the moment you were conceived to the present moment, your life has been changing. Cycle upon cycle of growth has passed through your days—so much life, so much death. The cycle goes on. I long for you to embrace each new growing season. I want you to experience the passion of abundant life. Between the rising and the setting sun you live the seasons of your life.

Be attentive to my fruitfulness. Listen to my growing and continue to reflect on your own potential for growth. There is a fruitfulness about your life that you've not fully discovered. Implant your roots deep into your heart's good soil where a treasure of nourishment waits for you. The roots of all that grows and thrives in my season have gone down deep searching for streams of water to assist their growth. You must do the same if you are to ripen and mature. Reach for that which will help you develop into a mature summer person with purpose and strength.

Reflect on your roots. They keep you grounded. Give them an image and call them by name: hope, faith, patience, joy, enthusiasm, gratitude, determination, endurance. Add others to this list. Envision these roots spreading through your good soil, enabling your summer-like growth.

Believe in your root system. You have growing power in you. Enjoy the process. Let the roots of your growth reach out to the world on lovely greening tendrils. Play a little each day in the fields of your life. Enter into the abundance of the summer within you and around you. Be attentive. Use your five senses to help you live fully.

Ponder these questions and live slowly into the answers.

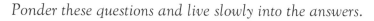

- How would you describe the fruitfulness of your life?

- Who or what is a source of growth for you?

- When are you most able to acknowledge your fruitfulness and taste its truth?

- In this season of abundance what is ripening in you?

- As you sit in the lap of summer is there any piece of growing that needs your attention?

- What are the names you would give to your central root system?

- If you were to choose a scripture passage that would be a summer text for you, what would it be?

Autumn Speaks

....

Earth is turning its face away from the sun. The vibrancy and energetic spirit of summer is waning. Your green playground is about to lose its bright colors. I am the season of surrender. Do not let your heart be afraid of the gifts I bring. I extend a mellow welcome to all who enter my world. I offer each person the plentitude of harvest. Those who take the time to sit under the archway of my wisdom will begin to perceive their life with greater clarity.

Death is no longer something they resist. They find comfort in my falling leaves and browning land because they recognize that this, too, is just one more piece of the never-ending circle of life. Those who develop a friendship with me begin to understand that my relinquishment of summer is not a final farewell to fruitfulness and growth. It is a transitional handing over of a life that needs to be protected and restored so it may stir anew in future seasons.

It is in the art of letting go that you truly come to life. Like all great art this surrender is the work of a lifetime. It requires diligent, faithful practice crowned with trust. Every day you are *dying to live* although you do not always recognize this. I understand your longing for permanence. It challenges me, too, when the leaves first begin to fall from the trees. There is a strong pull in all of life for security and stability. It is not easy to be strongly invested in life and yet remain unattached to it.

Learn from me the art of surrender. You, too, have leaves that must be shed so that you may be renewed. Learn to recognize your own dying leaves, your own crumbling foliage waiting to become rich soil for some new seed. You are part of a marvelous web of existence in which each part is held in the compassionate hands of the Creator.

 Lean into the mystery of the unknown. You will find enriching poetry there. It is a magical, mystical land. Just as you stand between the rising and setting sun, so, too, you stand between death and life. Each holds you by the hand. In their loving embrace you will find the path of ongoing renewal that is necessary for your daily growth.

Life does not stand still. It flows like a river. Water without an outlet soon becomes stagnant, making us vulnerable to disease. A life that stands still also becomes stagnant. Change is the one thing we can depend on. It is a constant. I invite you to accept change. All things are transitory. Honor that which is invisible and bow to all that comes wrapped in mystery. When I put an end to your summer glory, nostalgia often comes to nest in your soul. And yet, held in infinitely compassionate hands you are being led into the territory of unknowing. Surrender! Trust the grace that is carrying you.

Ponder these autumn questions and remember that reflection on the question is, in itself, a prayer.

- What are the leaves that must fall from your life in order for you to experience greater transformation?
- In what ways have you encountered change the past year?
- What needs to be harvested in your spiritual life?
- As you look back into your life, what were your great moments of surrender?
- What is most difficult to turn loose, e.g., opinions, possessions, etc.?
- In a society that makes aging look like a disease, what are your thoughts on the beauty of aging?
- If you were to choose a scripture passage with an autumn theme, what text would you choose?

Winter Speaks

Autumn spoke to you about the art of letting go, inviting you to surrender. Now I want to encourage you to relax in the midst of the surrender so that your letting go might be a joyous learning experience rather than a laborious task. You are one of God's holy and mysterious, grace-filled seeds. Would you like to rest in the quiet earth of your inner self? I can teach you to be silent and hopeful as you wait. You will learn this art if you are willing to slow down and observe my wisdom.

Be patient with each moment. You cannot hurry transformation. Allow it to unfold in its own time. As you learn to embrace my winter spirit you will discover there is an immense need for slowing down, for silence and resting. Carve out some time for solitude. Listen to all those things that speak without words. You do not always have to be producing, creating, harvesting. Learn to be idle. Learn to rest.

I spend long months in stillness. Those who observe me often think there is nothing happening in my great solitude and long nights of darkness. These people have obviously never lived inside my womb, for there they would find seeds growing strong for their spring journey. They would hear seeds dreaming. They would hear the sigh of the soil as it rests from its labors. They would be in awe of the wonders stirring inside my darkness.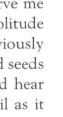

Let the image of my barren trees come into the eye of your heart. Notice the loveliness of the dark branches and the way they reach out in all directions. Look at their textures and shapes. This is my winter dance of emptiness, and I have come to treasure it. I am being renewed. I have gone into my dreaming time. Now, in my barrenness, a different kind of beauty is being revealed.

You, too, can discover beauty in the midst of your barrenness. Imagine that you are standing out there with the lonely trees. You have been stripped of all your bright knowing. You are empty and you are lonely. Do not be afraid of loneliness. In the heart of that loneliness you will discover your great need for God and for others. Find a winter tree. Stand beside it in its winter watch. Keep it company. Discover its beauty. Listen to its wordless sermon. Put your ear to my frozen ground and listen to the seeds as they dream.

Snuggle up in your prayer shawl and ponder these winter questions.

- Where do you find silence in your life?

- When do you feel free from the pressure to produce?

- What are the most challenging aspects of winter for you?

- How is the prayer of contemplation a part of your life?

- What have you discovered during your barren seasons?

- What can you do to provide the creative space that you need for yourself?

- If you were to choose a passage from scripture that speaks to you of winter, what would it be?

A Litany for the Seasons

Oseasons that circle our lives, you are God's holy messengers. You are the glory of the Creator written on Earth's face. O seasons that circle our lives, let your winds and breezes blow wide the doorway of our hearts and teach us. For deep within our beings the same wild eruption of life breaks forth in us each year: dangerous and beautiful, passionate and placid, changing and unchanging. We move through the waters of life inebriated with our own seasonal stories. All this unfolding! All this grace! Springs and summers! Autumns and winters! Teach us.

Spring

Spring Showers . . . Response: Teach Us Joy

Awakening Earth . . .

Morning Dew . . .

Nests of Robins . . .

Young Green Leaves .

Unfolding Petals . . .

Singing Seeds . . .

Opening Buds . . .

Nourishing Soil . . .

Greening Forests . . .

Glistening Moss . . .

Refreshing Raindrops . . .

Enthusiastic Winds . . .

Eastern Skies . . .

Summer

Summer Storms . . . Response: Teach Us Passion
Flowering Meadows . . .
Singing Birds . . .

Lakeside Picnics . . .
Outdoor Play . . .
Firefly Evenings . . .
Ripening Season . . .

Long Days of Light . . .
Fruitful Gardens . . .
Spectacular Blossoms . . .

Crickets Chanting . . .

Fiery Sun . . .
Southern Lands . . .

Autumn

Autumn Colors . . . Response: Teach Us Wisdom
Morning Frost . . .
Falling Leaves . . .
Hunter's Moon . . .
Fields of Grain . . .

Bountiful Harvest . . .
Softening Sunshine . .
Transient Beauty . . .
Enriching Compost . . .
Migrating Birds . . .
Death and Dying . . .
Flowing Waters . . .
Western Sunsets . . .

Winter

Winter Silence . . . Response: Teach Us Stillness
Barren Trees . . .
Bold Blue Skies . . .
Dancing Snowflakes . . .
Frosty Mornings . . .
Snow-Covered Fields . . .
Cold Winter Nights . . .
Quiet Energy . . .
Frozen Earth . . .
Months of Darkness . . .
Sleeping Seeds . . .
Stones of Strength . . .
Northern Lights . . .

Dear seasons that pass over our fields and through our hearts, you are the word of God spoken to us from the cathedral of the great outdoors. Stir up our love for life. Fill us with joy and passion, wisdom and stillness. Reveal to us our own endurance, patience, and ability to trust. Lead us into reflection and solitude as we move through the years held in the arms of mystery. Teach us to say "Yes" to the unfolding work of the Creator in our lives. Amen.

Seasons of an
Old Oak Tree

There is history underneath my bark. There is memory in my roots. I am old now, wiser than when I was an acorn hidden in the ground by a squirrel who obviously forgot about me. Many seasons have passed through my branches. I hold the memories like an old journal with precious and crumbling pages.

Oh, the many changes that have passed through my magnificent body. I remember autumn's crisp breath as one by one my leaves began to turn. People would contemplate me and photograph me. Although I wasn't quite so luminous as the neighboring maple, whose leaves often got stuck in my branches, I was a natural when it came to making people gaze in wonder. After autumn's breath became frosty my leaves turned brown. Slowly they fell to the ground except for the few that hung on until spring. I watched the people who once lived in my shade. With my leaves scattered to the farthest corners of the farm, I was grateful they wouldn't be needing my shade for a while.

I could feel mysterious changes within my body. Stormy winds swept through my branches and almost stripped me bare. Sheets of rain rushed through me and saturated the ground below. When the rains fell upon me, I soaked in all that moisture knowing I must hold it in my body for when the dry season returned. Then the air would grow brisk, clear and invigorating. In this great movement of transformation I knew that I was not the only one affected by this change of season. Hearts changed too. I witnessed the joys and sorrows of these hearts. And as I grew older, the family grew as well.

When smoke began rising from the chimney of the old farmhouse I knew the children wouldn't be playing in my branches for a while. I remember the first snowfall of each season when the snow covered my barren branches. The ice sometimes became a burden, bending my branches to the breaking point. I saw the challenge that winter's breath brought to the family who lived beside me—*my family* I liked to call them.

There was a certain beauty about me in my barrenness. Without my leaves I made spectacular silhouettes in the winter sunsets. My branches created artistic shadows in the waning sunlight. Around the base of my trunk I observed the work of art made by little tracks of rabbits, squirrels, and birds as they searched for food. After my leaves returned to the earth, there were spaces between my branches where the stars looked right through me on clear nights. Each season as winter moved into spring, I remember the feelings of the budding process. Even my root system knew something wondrous was happening in the cells beneath my bark. The few leaves I had clung to were finally pushed off as the pale green foliage began to form, and budding shoots pushed their way out.

I was especially moved by the wonder I caused, the joy I brought as I heard the children and the adults talk about my loveliness. The new life unfolding in me seemed to help them unfold as well. One by one my leaves came back. As my leaves matured and my foliage became brighter and thicker, the birds started to build nests in me again. I was very proud to be their tree house. They filled my limbs with song. In the distance I saw my family dropping seeds into the garden soil. Small wild flowers adorned the yard around me. Glorious is the only word I can think of to describe the festival of life that surrounded me each spring.

Ever so slowly I became a summer tree. There was a lot of activity then. The rope swing that one of my large branches held was busy delighting the children, and although the rope cut through the wood of my branches I didn't mind the slight discomfort as I beheld the happiness I brought. I felt the bare feet of children climbing through my branches, and I was glad. This, too, was part of living and giving and loving. I was bringing joy to others. With my leaves, now full and hearty, I was able to give shade again. At the noon hour the farm folk would often sit in my shade and lean against my trunk while they ate their lunch. I was so glad to be able to shelter them. Sometimes I prayed they would learn how to shelter one another.

 With my thousands of eyes, I watched all the summer activity. In the distance there was gardening, planting, hoeing, waiting, gathering. After a long work day there were evenings when night returned and the children raced through the darkness surrounded by fireflies. Sometimes the hoot owl would sit in my branches and join me in prayer, hooting out her secret wisdoms to the family in the house.

All through the years I beheld transforming circles of life moving through me: crisp autumn weather, the surrender of my leaves, the frosty breath of winter, bitter cold winds, my barren body silhouetted in the sunsets, my roots warming both sleeping seeds and insects, soft sunlight thawing the ground, the melting of snow, the feel of new life pulsing through my branches, the budding process, the great opening, the blossoming all around me, the delight of spring raindrops—and then the summer-green leaves when once again it was possible for me to give shade, the wonderful fruitfulness, the thickening of the grasses, the locusts' song vibrating through my branches, fireflies darting around my trunk, the ripening of the gardens. I weathered it all. Now I am old. My family is gone but, oh, how well I remember the energy we exchanged. In that brief time they were part of the circle of my life, and I grew strong in the circle of their love.

MACRINA WIEDERKEHR

Where Do Poems Live?

I n the heart of winter you will find them buried deep in the beautiful rest of non-action. The seed in the soil knows them by heart. The first snowflakes of the season herald them. They rise up out of your breath on frosty mornings and burn logs in your fireplace as the day begins and ends. They gather for stories at the kitchen table. They live in the heart of the storyteller and watch for tears and smiles on the faces of the listeners. As the sun rises over your rooftop they are there, and after it sets they take a very short nap, then build their tents in the darkness and wait for the stars to appear. When the cold air outside companions the warmth on the inside, they etch themselves onto the glass of the frosty windowpanes. The barren trees, arms raised in praise, sing of their glory, and the bright winter sunsets birth them each evening.

Where do poems live?

When spring shows her face you find them awaiting her arrival. They rise up out of the winter ground, laughing like children set free from school. They hide in opening buds as surprises are about to be unveiled. They live in the chlorophyll that paints the trees and grasses green. They spend much of their time in gardens. When you gather vegetables for your dinner table they follow you into the house. They climb into the serving bowls on your dinner table and dream of nourishing you with vitality and energy. They fall on your land in raindrops, and the storms that toss you about are not strangers to their presence. The wild flowers are among poems' finest children and the mockingbird sings of them day and night. The fruit trees inscribe them on its branches in the form of blossoms. They kneel with you by your bedside when you pray your prayers at the end of day.

Where do poems live?

Summer holds them in its deep green branches and birds sing them right out of the sky. They ride on the wings of the swallows. They hang in the feathers of the hawk searching for food. The orchards heavy with fruit sing of their presence. The fireflies in the meadows light up their way. The summer lakes and happy children's voices ripple with their music. The cows in the bright green field look like poems to the wise ones. And the ones who milk the cows are milking poems. The cardinal's song is a lovely poem. And when your cat brings you the gift of a bird, even that is a bittersweet poem. The night songs of little forest creatures feed them to you in the evening. And the night sky wraps you with memories of them when you dream.

Where do poems live?

When autumn shows its face they are present with their greetings. They live in all that prepares for hibernation. When death claims us as its own, they stand there beside us with their secrets. They are present in wrinkled, aging faces and hearts full of stories. Autumn leaves slowly changing into glorious colors speak silently of their presence. They are seen flying by your window in the shape of fallen leaves. And when the leaves are raked into heaps in your yard, even then they are not hidden. They sing brown crumbling songs from each pile of leaves. Children make visible the hidden poems when they roll delightfully in the autumn leaves and wear them in their hair. Geese flying south carry poems on their wings. And the people who take time to watch the geese bring them into their hearts to rest.

MACRINA WIEDERKEHR

Where Are the Safe Seasons?

Out of the forest,
one by one, they come:
vigilant, fearful, and lovely,
bright piercing eyes
scanning their spacious dining hall.

The table of the earth holds
the golden grain scattered
for their evening meal.

Gathering at that table
the ritual begins.
They eat, dancing
a dance of caution,
like sentinels on the watch

lest some enemy
harm the loveliness of their being,
heads bobbing up and down,
guarded, aloof, alert,
ready to dance back into the forest
at the slightest disturbance.

Barely moving a muscle
I sit in silence
watching the dance of graceful caution.

Catching my eye
a little doe lifts her foot in the air

then touches the earth with determination,

another step of the dance,

a ritual proclaiming,

"This is my space, my dining hall, my dance floor."

Gazing with respect, love, and wonder,

a tiny sadness surges through me

as I remember how I, too,

have learned steps to a fearful dance,

casting glances over my shoulder,

not quite at ease in my being,

always yearning for a safer season,

ready to dance back into my forest of protection.

Where are the safe seasons?

Do you know?

MACRINA WIEDERKEHR

Bread for the Seasons

Bread remembers, and if it could talk, it would say:

Come to me and taste God—salty as the river of our blood,

sweet as honey and apricots, smoother than oil, stronger than death.

NATHAN MITCHELL

This service is designed for circles of women throughout the world who want to break bread together, women whose powers and gifts are often overlooked in the institutional church. Sensitive, insightful men will also find meaning in this bread service. This is but one suggestion. Hopefully, it will inspire other creative ways to celebrate the breaking and bonding of our lives as we search for new ways to sanctify the wondrous workings of the Spirit.

The Setting

On the table in the center of the room four candles have been placed corresponding to the four directions:

> *Winter—a blue candle,*
>
> *Spring—a green candle,*
>
> *Summer—a yellow candle,*
>
> *Autumn—an orange/rust candle.*

Begin with a song of your choice.

The Lighting of the Four Seasons Candles

Assign candle lighters to hold up the designated candle on the table for each direction as the blessing is proclaimed.

We light this candle in honor of spring, season of resurrection, with its vibrant renewal of life. We honor everything within us that is eager to announce the story of hope and rebirth. May the creatures of this world joyfully echo spring's song of promise and renewal.

We light this candle in honor of summer, season of fruitfulness, with its passion for abundance and growth. We honor everything within us that is willing to lean toward the light. May the creatures of this world grow bright with the fire of summer's growth.

We light this candle in honor of autumn, season of harvest with its invitation to gather our wisdom. We honor all within us that is willing to listen to our dreams and visions. May the creatures of this world be robed in the bright colors of autumn transformation.

We light this candle in honor of winter, season of faith, with its long dark nights that call us into solitude. We honor all within us that is willing to wait for renewal. May the creatures of this world grow strong in the womb of winter's silence.

Reading

A reading of your choice is now read, followed by a period of silence.

This Is My Body

The French priest Pierre Teilhard de Chardin, who at one time was silenced by the church for his teachings, was not able to celebrate Mass when he was out in the Ordos desert in China. Many women will be able to identify with the sentiments in the following prayer that he prayed. Listen carefully to the words of this prayer.

Since once again . . . I have neither bread, nor wine, nor altar,

I will raise myself beyond these symbols, up to the pure

majesty of the real itself; I, your priest, will make the whole

earth my altar. . . . Over every living thing which is to spring up,

to grow, to flower, to ripen during this day, say again the words:

This is my body.

PIERRE TEILHARD DE CHARDIN
"THE MASS ON THE WORLD" FROM *Hymn of the Universe*

All are now invited to go outdoors and experience the amazing reality of our oneness with God. Send them forth with the following words:

Behold the earth, trees, sky, flowers, ground, rocks, whatever crosses your path. Touch all that you see. Be a listening presence. Hear these words spoken to you and through you over and over again: This is my body.

When the group returns a loaf of bread will be at the center of the table with four empty baskets representing the four directions. Luke 24:28–35, The Road to Emmaus, is read.

The leader breaks the bread into four pieces, placing the pieces in the baskets. As the leader reads the following blessing prayers, four people, previously assigned, will offer the bread to each direction as the prayer is prayed.

Bread Offering Prayers

Bread is offered to the east; all extend a hand toward the east.

> Bread of the East: Home of the rising sun,
>
> broken that we may be hope for the world.

Bread is offered to the south; all extend a hand toward the south.

> Bread of the South: Home of the fire within,
>
> broken that our lives may be a passionate

outpouring of love for the world.

Bread is offered to the west; all extend a hand toward the west.

> Bread of the West: Home of the setting sun
>
> broken that we might learn to honor the death in our lives
>
> that is being transformed into wells of wisdom for our world.

Bread is offered to the north; all extend a hand toward the north.

> Bread of the North: Home of the sleeping seed,
>
> broken that we may learn to be obedient
>
> to what needs solitude and rest in us.

Bread is offered to the heavens; all extend a hand toward the heavens.

> Bread of the Heavens: Home of the Great Spirit
>
> broken that we may learn to honor the Divine in us.

Bread is offered to Earth; all extend a hand downward toward Earth.

> Bread of Earth: Home of the sacred waters,
>
> broken that we may learn to be grateful
>
> for the Womb of our Mother.

Bread is offered to the center; all turn to the center and extend a hand toward the bread.

> Bread of Our Lives: Home of the Tree of Life,
>
> broken that we may learn to honor the center of our
> being, that place from which Christ rules the world.

Participants now come forward in pairs to the four corners of the table. Each breaks off a piece of bread and offers it to the other person. (An appropriate response might be: "We are the Body of Christ.") After all have shared, sit for a time of silence.

Closing Prayer

Gracious Sustainer of Life, we have broken and shared this bread with hope in our hearts. May that day dawn when all peoples of the world can gather around the one table of Earth and feed one another without fear. As we leave this gathering may we remember and celebrate what we have experienced here. As we return to our homes may we carry with us hearts refreshed and renewed with your sanctifying presence.

Conclude with a song of your choice.

Lighting the Four Seasons Candle

We light this candle for our springtime hearts,
for that season when hope raises her head
and turns our eyes toward the great blossoming:
for the greening in the meadows,
for the sunrise of new birth,
for the thawing of the frozen land,
for the newly planted seeds.
May all our springtime stories rise up and bless us,
singing out songs of gladness.

We light this candle for our summer hearts,
for that season when the sunny side of life embraces us:
for time to relax, for vacations,
for each part of our life that is wakeful and fruitful,
for gardens outside and the gardens of our hearts,
for resting in the shade of the fullness of growth,
for all within us that keeps raising its face to the sun.
May all our summer stories rise up and bless us,
anointing us with the goodness of abundant life.

We light this candle for our autumn hearts,
for that season when Earth turns away from the sun:
for the transformation taking place throughout the
    land,
for the eternal mystery that surrounds our lives,
for the falling leaves of our transitions,

for the diminishing energy of bodies and spirits,
for the great recycling taking place in the earth.
May all our autumn stories rise up to bless us,
reminding us of our many life-giving deaths.

We light this candle for our winter hearts,
for that season when darkness covers the land:
for all that rests beneath the frozen ground,
for the hope that waits in our own iced-in spaces,
for the long nights of emptiness when our faith is made
    strong,
for the songs of wisdom, born in the silent places,
for our contemplative hearts fashioned in holy
    darkness.
May all our winter stories rise up to bless us,
reminding us of the light that shines on in the darkness.

A Seasonal Journey With Wheat

Each of the four seasons
is a growing season for the heart.
If you sink your roots deeply
into the soil of each season's truth,
it can become your mentor.

MACRINA WIEDERKEHR

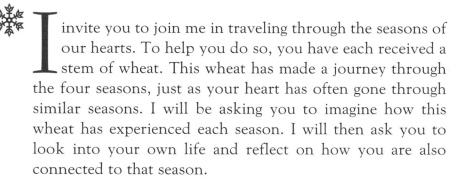

Each participant receives a stem of wheat (or rye or oats). Participants will be walking with their stem of wheat unless there is not enough space for all to do so. If this is the situation, have them sit or stand in place instead. The leader begins:

I invite you to join me in traveling through the seasons of our hearts. To help you do so, you have each received a stem of wheat. This wheat has made a journey through the four seasons, just as your heart has often gone through similar seasons. I will be asking you to imagine how this wheat has experienced each season. I will then ask you to look into your own life and reflect on how you are also connected to that season.

We are going to be walking through each season. As I speak I will ask you to hold the wheat in a way that symbolizes how it experienced that season. You will begin walking with the wheat. Then I will ask you to pause, to stop walking and stand still. During this time you will be reflecting on your own experience of each season.

Winter

Hold the stem of seeds flat in your two open palms.

Begin walking very slowly.

Look at the stem of seeds, lying there in your hand, quiet and waiting. . . .

Remember winter and the fallowness of this season, when all seemed dead and unavailable to life. . . .

The seed that took root grew and produced the stem of wheat you hold now. . . .

It was once a tiny, dry, shrunken seed in the dark soil.

Stop walking now and stand still in place.

Remember your own winter times when all seemed dead and unavailable to life,

when you wanted to give up hope and stop believing. . . .

Is there any place in your life that currently feels like winter?

Greet this winter part of yourself with compassion. . . .

Pray for a strong and enduring faith. . . .

Spring

Hold the stem of seeds straight up in the air.

Begin walking again.

Look at the wheat and imagine how its original seed was in springtime,

how sunlight and rain awakened it . . . coaxed it out of its dry shell. . . .

Imagine how it grew into greenness . . . how it became a sturdy stem . . .

growing straight and tall. . . .

Stop walking now and stand still in place.

Think of spring and how it has so much energy that it pushes new life through the strong soil, like a baby pushing through the birth canal of a mother. . . .

Remember how newness has come to your life through love relationships, spiritual growth, renewed hope, and health and other experiences. . . .

What is now waiting to be birthed in you?

Send encouragement to this part of you.

Summer

Sway the stem of seeds back and forth slowly.

Begin walking again.

Imagine a field full of wheat in the brilliant sunlight. . . .

Look at the stems growing taller, swaying in the summer wind. . . .

Notice how they are forming seeds of grain . . . plump and full of life.

Stop walking now and stand still in place.

Think of summer and how fields and gardens are fruitful and abundant. . . .

Remember your summertime, the successes of your life, the times of vast growth. . . .

Recall the moments of joy and enthusiasm . . .
of peace and contentment. . . .

What is seeming most like summer in your life right
now?

Offer gratitude for this part of your life.

Autumn

Take one seed off of your stem of seeds and give it to
someone.

Begin walking again.

Feel the dryness of the stem with seeds.

Look at the sharp cut at the bottom of the stem. . . .

Imagine a field full of grain,

ripe and golden, ready to be harvested. . . .

What does the land experience as threshers cut down
ripened stems full of grain?

How is it that Earth shares her abundance so
generously?

How naturally she yields and accepts the letting go that
is required in this process.

Stop walking now and stand still in place.

Think of autumn in your life.

What has been given? What has been taken?

When have you had times of greater darkness and
lesser illumination?

Are you needing to yield and give away, to let go, in
some part of your life?

Open your mind and heart to the undesired changes
that are required of you.

Hold the stem full of seeds close to your heart now.

This wheat has experienced the circle of life.

There is wisdom to be gleaned in each season.

Quietly thank the stem of wheat for journeying with you as you reflected on your life.

Take time now to write about this experience in your notebook. (The following questions may be helpful.)

Questions for internal reflection

1. Which season is most predominant in my life now?

2. What are my strongest thoughts and feelings about each season?

   (Write a thought and a feeling for each of these seasons. Or draw . . . or dance. . . .)

3. Which season has taught me the most in regard to my relationship with the Holy One?

4. What are some of these teachings or wisdoms? (List them in your journal.)

5. Which season is most appealing to me? Why?

6. Which season is least appealing to me? Why?

7. What is most challenging for me when I look at the four seasons of my spiritual life?

Integration

Hold the stem of seeds in your hands. Be still. Listen attentively. Place the stem of seeds beside your journal. Write a letter to this stem of seeds.

Storms of the
Four Seasons

The four seasons are wonderful inventions of the Creator. They bring humankind much diversity, joy, and satisfaction. What these four seasons also bring are stormy times. No matter where we live on this planet, no matter what season, it is impossible to avoid a weather disturbance now and then. Clouds gather. Thunderstorms brew. Winds pick up speed. Dust storms develop. Hailstones fall from the dark sky. Lightning bolts strike without warning.

Sometimes these storms are fierce. Floods, tornadoes, hurricanes, and blizzards can be fatal for those caught in them. Human limbs and lives can be permanently altered by destructive seasonal outbursts. Family mementos and treasures are flung away and destroyed. Well-loved homes are washed into the sea, vegetable and grain fields inundated with rain. Old, sturdy trees are ripped out by their roots. In a brief moment, land and lives can be changed forever.

Fierce storms scare us, intrigue us, and astound us all at the same time. Some storms bring with them an amazing beauty. Damaging, freezing rain glazes the world with glassy elegance. Ferocious winds, with their wildness and passionate freedom, stir the human heart. Jagged lightning in the night sky offers a natural laser show. Dark, ominous clouds are mountains of amazing power. Swirling snowstorms create artistic patterns on sidewalks and windowsills.

There are also those storms that move in just long enough to cause anxiety and concern. They never develop into much. If they do, they leave nary a scratch of damage on anything or anyone. Still, any storm is unpredictable and

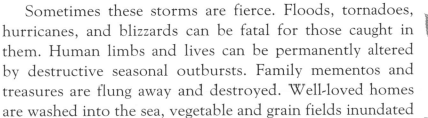

is to be respected. They don't always come in an acceptable and expected time. Many a person has been caught in a springtime snowstorm just when they were sure that winter was long gone.

 What is true for seasonal storms on the planet is also true for the storms that stir in our personal lives. After some unsettling encounters we can start up again the next day and quickly forget they ever happened. Other stormy situations stay with us for years, reminding us, not by scars on the external landscape, but by the scars on our heart.

 There are storms that come unexpectedly with a diagnosis of serious illness, a homicide, a violent accident. These human storms can come just as unexpectedly, just as fiercely, as weather patterns come. And they cause just as much damage. These human storms bash and batter our joy and our self-confidence. They flood us with depression, anxiety, and dread. Some personal storms whip us around so intensely with constant change and loss that we wonder if we will be able to make it through the turmoil.

 Persons who have known the storm of divorce, cancer, job loss, or financial failure sometimes spend years picking up the pieces of their lives. It can take a long time to rebuild a house destroyed by a tornado. It can take much longer to rebuild a heart destroyed by betrayal, a loved one's death, or any other significant loss.

Can there be beauty in our fierce, stormy disturbances? No one would consider something beautiful if it rips security, safety, health, happiness, and well-being away from them. Yet within these storms there may still lie some hidden beauty: human care and concern, the amazing power of faithful love, generous help, compassionate understanding. Our personal storms may hold the beauty of discovery: recognition of what truly counts in one's life, finding new courage, learning to let others enter into our heart, or identifying a hidden talent.

The teaching that the seasonal storms of Earth bring to us is that we cannot get through life without at least a few strong tempests. Some storms may be predictable, but with others we will be caught off guard. We will occasionally be battered by the fierceness of our personal storms. We will often have to clean up the mess they leave. It can be a daunting task. Always, we will need time to recover emotionally. It will take patience to slowly put our lives back together again.

Even the most severe weather does not last forever. So, too, with our personal storms. After our human turbulence, there is an eventual return of light and peace. We need to trust reality. When the damage from our storms seems too much to endure peace will come again.

Spring

A
Season
of
Birthing

Introduction
to Spring

··

Listen! In the earth, the seeds are stirring and making noise, like the birds whose song has been silenced by winter. Now the snow is being devoured by sun, our elder, and in the branches, the persistence of our prayers is bringing the birds to life.

NANCY WOOD, SHAMAN'S CIRCLE

When the season of spring returns to the land, a festival of life and light abounds. Suddenly, there are longer days of sunlight, earlier dawns, later sunsets. Earth sails along in her faithful rotation. With each cycle, she leans in closer to the light and heat of the life-giving sun. Windy breezes fill the air with an odor of freshness. What once appeared dead begins to stir. Each wintered thing wakes up, raises its drowsy head, and sniffs the air to confirm the truth of spring's arrival. The slow pace of winter is left behind and there is a surge of invigorating activity for humans, creatures, and vegetation.

As spring arrives, the creatures that have hidden in the dark folds of winter's skirts are lured by the light and warmth of the penetrating sun. Bird songs echo with mating calls. Woodchucks shuffle along in the rain, glad to be above ground again. Mother bears nudge their little cubs to explore the intriguing life unfolding before them. Fish begin to move through thawed waters. It is a jubilant time for nature. Freedom is in the air.

The tantalizing rains of spring and the convincing rays of sunshine are too enticing for nature to resist. Delicate green shoots triumphantly push their way through the remnants of winter's long stay. Everywhere there is evidence of spring's entrance. There is much to marvel at: tiny seeds in newly warmed soil shed their husks; thick walled bulbs open their protective doors to allow future flowers to step out; shrubs and trees model their emerging leaves. Each nook and cranny of earth explodes with life.

One can almost hear the voice of this birthing season calling: "Now! Now! Now is the time to resurrect!" Fields and forests are filled with newly born creatures. Fronds of fern unfold. Grasses rise up out of the earth, strong and tall. After months of drab grays and bleak browns, brilliant color returns to the land. Bright faced tulips, hyacinths, and daffodils herald the advent of the season. Beautiful blossoms of redbud, magnolia, and cherry trees sway with joy in the spring breezes. The hills and valleys become a palette filled with shades of meadow green, mossy green, leafy green, forest green, grassy green, ivy green.

While spring is a time of intense growth, it is also a time to refresh, clean, and empty out the clutter that has collected during the sedentary months. Cars are washed and waxed; windows are opened to get rid of stale air; gardens are cleared for planting; newly grown lawns are mowed; closets and basements are divested of their refuse.

Spring has its shadow side. Its fragrant, colorful blossoms can give rise to irritating allergies. Sudden warmth often melts snow too quickly. Unending rains may overwhelm saturated soil, causing severe flooding. Seasonal currents of change can spawn tornadoes, bring damaging winds or hailstorms. Vibrancy and fresh beginnings of growth, however, are what dominate spring. These lively energies awaken and move through the heart of creation.

The human spirit also experiences seasons of springtime. The periods of depression and discouragement that visit our inner landscape do not last forever. Like rays of sun breaking through storm clouds, currents of hope flow through the dark walls of despondency. Blessings arise as new growth takes place. At first, we may not trust this stirring of life within, especially if our winter sojourn has been intense and lengthy. Doubt and hesitation may fight against the buds of hope trying to break through. The spirit of renewal is strong, however, and eventually it gently takes over the heart.

It sometimes happens that one's spirit is so wintered and frozen that it cannot enter the season of spring without some assistance. Just as a gardener is helpful in complementing and assisting the great work that nature has done in the soil, so too, a very broken spirit may need a gardener of the soul, a counselor to companion it into new growth.

In the heart's springtime, the inner self awakens. Seeds of growth, hidden in the midst of winter's bleakness, germinate and sprout. That which has been longed for and greatly desired is gradually brought forth and heralded with gladness. Visions, dreams, and yearnings for the future unfold. The gray moods, the frozen love, the sorrow and grief, the overwhelming angst, the dread and depression, all this slowly slips away as trust and enthusiasm rejuvenate the wintered spirit. Like the springtime land, so the inner land is thawed and re-energized. A sense of loving and being loved warms the interior places that were cold and dormant in wintertime.

The emotional clutter and the old debris that prevented clear thinking are cleansed. Spaciousness and openness expand like the wings of a great swan. Inner freedom is discovered. Confidence returns. Creative endeavors begin to emerge. Like the songbirds chirping as they return from the south, the heart begins to sing again.

The interior spring stretches the human spirit toward growth the way the sun stretches plants. This inner movement can come about with a new job bringing affirmation and assurance of one's abilities. The new start could come from a successful surgery, a restored relationship, or a decision to let go of an old hurt. It might be something totally unexpected like a taste of joy rising up, presenting itself as clearly as the first colorful face of a crocus smiling in the snow. Never did the human spirit believe it could feel so happy or be so immersed in the goodness of life.

There are times when spring enters the heart dramatically. An unexpected insight can bring about immense clarity and encouraging self-revelation. A song, a vivid dream, a piece of poetry, meeting a kindred spirit, a walk through the woods can become a beautiful inner rising akin to a resurrection experience. When these spring-like encounters take place, our inner search is blessed with a new and invigorating sense of purpose and direction.

The momentum of birthing and the vibrancy of life pulse everywhere. In this season of the soul, there is awe and wonder at the changes taking place. Spring generates surprise, delight, unmitigated joy, and newly found optimism. Now is the time to enjoy what is emerging from within, to savor the taste of hope, and to trust in what the future promises. It is the time to believe in growth and to give oneself to it wholeheartedly.

Like all seasons, spring will not stay forever. It will pass into summer where another dimension of growth will reveal itself. Every season's entrance and departure is part of the great turning of the circle of life. Spring will return to the heart when it is time.

Spring Flowers

Last night after sunset
I put my flower children to bed,
covered their cheery pink faces
with blankets, towels, and sheets,

said, "Goodnight, stay warm,
don't let the frost-bugs bite,"
hoping, when I arose next day,
that the long cold night
had not nipped their spring noses
and frightened them to death.

How carefully I care
for the small flower garden,
protecting all I can from harm.
Yet, when the green shoots
of my own inner growth
push their way out,
I seem to leave all to chance
and little to care.

I wonder why.

JOYCE RUPP

Awakening

·······················

The world around me was drab and weary as I walked along the park trail the last week of February. Everything was smudged with grit and grayness. Not a trace of green. Not a snowflake left to cover the brown mush with a clean layer of white. Just brown, forlorn branches above me and earth soiled by the mushy gravy of old snow beneath me. Turning from the trail onto the sidewalk that led homeward, I plodded through little mounds of dirty sand, shoved there by snowplows when they had cleared the streets. More brown. More dirt. More dullness.

As I reached home, I looked at the matted brown lawn and the restless oak trees with their dry, tattered leaves still hanging on. Everything looks so ugly, I thought, recalling that Iowa almost always looks dreary before spring awakens. In late-winter bleakness I especially long for the freshness that spring rains bring. Try as I might, I can barely perceive any beauty in what I see around me during the time just before spring begins. All I can do is wait for the change to come. What a big hurrah it is when the first stems of green push their way up through the tired-looking ground.

This day, however, I tried to peer more deeply into the drabness, to see the inner story of the land's bedraggled appearance. As I did so, I noticed that the smeared and worn land was similar to what happens inside of me before inner awakenings occur. Often my spirit takes on a similar dingy and lifeless tone. During this dull period no creative energy stirs. My hopes and dreams sit like stones inside of me.

This is when I experience a type of *seasonal liminality*, a tedious, in-between space when I am no longer in the frozen stillness of winter but not yet in the surging energy of spring. The old saying about night being darkest just before dawn is an apt parallel here. The same sort of thing happens to my inner self. I feel like it's taking forever for spring to arrive as I sit in the doldrums of dullness.

My spirit in late February is like a pregnant woman in her last month, trying to manage the tediousness of her extra bulk, her emotions a ragged late-winter tree. As she yearns for the emptying of her womb and a regaining of her energy, she often feels unkempt and drab. Time weighs heavily as the weeks before her delivery gradually pass by.

When my inner world experiences the February blahs, the temptation is to fight, to struggle, to yell at the drabness, to try to figure a way out of it, to do anything to escape the endless monotony. Much patience is required before my inner landscape changes. Enormous acceptance of the process is asked of me before the greening begins.

Deep trust in unseen growth is absolutely necessary. Beneath the seeming ugliness and deadness, Earth's life is awakening. Inside the thick darkness of predawn, the sun is getting ready to rise. Within the pregnant woman, unborn life is receiving some finishing touches.

Why do I get so impatient for my inner springtime when it seems slow in arriving? Past experience tells me that eventually my weary dullness will move into enthusiasm and insight. Each year I see more clearly that I must be willing to pay the price of awakening: to wait without control of the process, to trust without seeing the face of the secret life that stirs, to hope without happy feelings, and to work with what seems to be little fruition.

The land waits. The dawn waits. The pregnant woman waits. I, too, must wait.

A Spring Blessing

Blessed are you, spring,
bright season of life awakening.
You gladden our hearts
with opening buds and returning leaves
as you put on your robes of splendor.

Blessed are you, spring.
In you is a life no death can destroy.
As you exchange places with winter
you harbor no unforgiving spirit
for broken tree limbs and frozen buds.

Blessed are you, spring.
You open the closed buds of our despair
as you journey with us
to the flowering places.

Blessed are you, spring.
You invite us to sing songs
to the frozen regions within
and to bless the lessons of winter
as we become your partner in a new dance.

Blessed are you, spring.
Like Jesus, standing before the tomb of Lazarus,
you call to us: "Remove winter's stone, come out,
there is life here you have not yet tasted."

Blessed are you, spring,
free gift of the earth.
Without cost we gaze upon your glory.
You are a gospel of good news
for the poor and rich alike.

Blessed are you, spring.
Your renewing rain showers and cathartic storms
nurture the potential that sleeps in Earth's heart
and in our own earthen hearts.

Blessed are you, spring,
season of resurrection, sacrament of promise.
Like Jesus you rise up out of the darkness,
leaving around you a wake of new life.

Blessed are you, spring,
miracle child of the four seasons.
With your wand of many colors
you work magic in the corners of our darkness.

Blessed are you, spring,
season of hope and renewal.
Wordless poem about all within us
that can never die.
Each year you amaze us
with the miracle of returning life.

Spring, a Season for Rising

I said to the almond tree:
Speak to me of God;
and the almond tree blossomed.

NIKOS KAZANTZAKIS

When I was growing up there was a spring cry in our household that equaled the holiness of the antiphons and chants we sing in church. What shall I call it? A mantra? No, a mantra is too quiet, too within—murmured in silence. This was a cry of pure delight. It was more like a gospel, a heralding of good news. It was a proclamation of spring.

And this was the cry, *The martins are back! The martins are back!* This was the clock that told us spring had returned. The swift purple martins would come in on wings of joy returning to their tall summer homes towering in the sky. Their return, whether it was before or after March 21, was the beginning of spring for us. Not quite as accurate as the swallows of Capistrano, perhaps, but faithful harbingers of spring all the same. It was a great homecoming. These swift circling birds of the swallow family brought much joy to my summer evenings. Their melodious trills filled my surroundings with music.

Just as joyful as the martins' return was the great blossoming that took place each spring. Mama always assured me that secrets hidden in the winter would surprise me in the spring; and she was right! About the time of the martins return, every tree, every bush and shrub, every flower, every blade of grass started telling the secret that was hidden in the hard crust of winter's earth. And what was the secret? Ah! The secret was *life*. All the gardens stayed busy proclaiming the gospel of life.

When I think of spring I think of *laughter*. Resurrection. Renewal. Easter. Birth. Rebirth. A joyful return of life is made visible in a myriad of ways. Little growing things start sticking their heads out of the ground. How can one refrain from smiling at a crocus? I remember a little poem by Lilia Royers that I memorized on a happy spring day that is now somewhere in my heart's archives.

> First a howling blizzard woke us,
>
> and then the rain came down to soak us:
>
> And now before our eye can focus,
>
> CROCUS!

It is easy to see this drama of life unfolding in the gardens and forests. However, we must look even closer. What about the garden of our hearts? How is the spirituality of spring bringing about a renewal in our personal life?

Although we are celebrating the return of spring and the resurrection of Jesus, this does not necessarily mean that our mood of life is the color of resurrection. In more ways than one, Easter is a movable feast. The Good Fridays of our lives do not always leave just because spring returns.

Spring is not a happy time for everyone. Many suicides take place in spring. There is such a vibrant call to life and renewal and joy that people who are depressed and lonely can suffer deeply because something wonderful is taking place outside their window and they do not feel invited. They cannot take part. When T. S. Eliot wrote "April is the cruelest month" in his famous poem "The Waste Land," he was in a dark depression. One of my friends, who dearly loved spring and wrote breathtakingly beautiful columns about nature in a country newspaper, took his life one April morning. Why? Somehow the terrible beauty and the terrible pain in his life didn't know how to be friends.

 Just because the season outside our window wears the face of spring doesn't mean that it's spring in the heart. It is highly possible that despite the festival of spring, despite life having a jubilee all around us, we can look on only with disdain.

Those who are depressed are not the only ones who have difficulty entering into the "festival of life." When we allow ourselves to be caught up in an abnormally fast pace of living, it is unlikely we will notice the festival of resurrection unfolding around us. Perhaps the wisest thing we can do if we are having a "winter of the heart" during spring is to sit down and offer hospitality to that wintered heart and ask if it has a teaching for us.

 During this season it is helpful to take a little time to meditate on the return of life. How are we, like the buds of the earth, opening to God and to others? What secrets buried deep in the soil of our soul are being revealed to us?

How is the gospel of springtime unfolding for us? What is the great blossoming in us?

When I am able to hear the voiceless invitation of the seasons of the earth, I am almost always called into prayer. I'm not referring to formal prayer but rather a natural prayer that rises spontaneously from a heart that has learned to listen to the moments. It is the prayer of being there. The seasons are more dear to me than any book I've read. Some unseen holy spirit turns the pages for me each year. My privilege is to be there. Being there is very easy and very difficult. Sometimes it's the easy tasks that are most difficult. The distractions that pull me away are many. The season of spring has a special ability to awaken me to joy, gratitude, and praise. The prayer of praise is an attitude of gratitude toward life. One of the things I've noticed about myself is that when I am grateful I feel almost impelled to reach out to others. I am pulled out of myself and long to find ways to bring joy to those around me. This prayer of praise fills me and surrounds me every spring. When I am connected with the beautiful, I feel called to give praise to the One from whom all this beauty has come.

MACRINA WIEDERKEHR

Praying With the Gospel of Spring

These passages from the gospel of John are suggestions for springtime praying. They are texts that portray the return of spring. They are springtime gospels.

1. Read and meditate on John 11:1–44.

    Lazarus, like an opening bud, comes out of the tomb. He is still bound but he is received back into the hands of the artists in the assembly. Gently they unbind him and set him free. Leaving death behind, he steps back into life.

    Spend time reflecting on a moment when you stepped out of the tomb of death and into the womb of life.

2. Read and meditate on John 20:10–18.

    Mary, weeping at the tomb, is experiencing the terrible darkness of the death of Jesus. She has not yet seen the hope that stands waiting in the garden. Then suddenly Jesus calls her by name and her winter leaps into spring.

    Recall a time when your name spoken was a gift of life. Who was it that spoke your name?

3. Read and meditate on John 5:1–9.

A nameless man is lying by the pool. Thirty-eight years is a very long winter. The gospel of spring was far away until he heard the question that was also an invitation: Do you want to be healed? Would you like to arise from your bondage and be set free? Take up your mat and go home.

And what about you? What is the mat of bondage that prevents you from leaping into a life of greater quality? What keeps you from leaping out of winter into spring?

O Antiphons for Spring

The O Antiphons have been assembled from various scriptural titles used for Christ; they are ancient prayers of longing in which the church expresses a desire for the coming of the Messiah. In this work we have written O Antiphons that express the human longing to be open to the truth that each new season brings.

O Midwife of Spring,

Come! Come encourage what needs to be born in us.
Draw us out of winter's nurturing womb.
Teach us to believe in our unopened buds.
Accompany us into a world starved for new life.
O Come!

O Seed Buried in the Soil,

Come! Come die to your seed-like condition.
Break through the darkness that has cradled your life.
Pierce the hard husk of all that we cling to.
Urge us to listen to the quiet sound of growing.
O Come!

O Hidden Life Now Unveiled,

Come! Come, welcome guest.
Set free our reluctance to live fully and deeply.
Awaken us to the beauty that holds and enfolds us.
Open our eyes to all we can become.
O Come!

O Spring Rising Out of Winter's Arms,

Come! Come melt what is frozen in us.
Open the buds of our longing with your gentle breezes.
Soften the hard earth of our hearts with your rains.
Breathe warmth upon the cold places in us.
O Come!

O Green Mantle of Creation,

Come! Come clothe us with the colors of spring.
Paint our fields and forests with your artist's brush.
Leap into our lives with a lover's enthusiasm.
Fill us with boundless energy and faithful hearts.
O Come!

O Child of Resurrection,

Come! Come dancing out of winter's gloom.
Enliven us with your radiant hope.
Lure us through the closed doors of our doubt.
Celebrate with us the wonder of risen life.
O Come!

O Laughter of the Earth,

Come! Come laugh us out of our rigidity.
Lighten hearts grown weary with anxiety.
Send us out to the meadows to play like a child.
Rise up in our souls with lighthearted joy.
O Come!

O Awakening Dawn,

Come! Come like the day star rising out of the east.
Come bearing the sparkling rays of your sunbeams.
Come carrying baskets of flowers and green-laced leaves.
Call forth blossoms sleeping in the garden of our lives.
O Come!

Everything Is Wet

W et,
everything is wet.

The birch trees are soaked
with great drops of moisture
rolling down their white chins.
Transparent rounds of rain
pull together at needle points,
creating shining mandalas
of beauty on the scotch pines.

Cardinals shake their wet wings
and fluff out red feathers,
unembarrassed about bathing
in such a public place.

The air is filled with dampness.
Furniture feels its sticky touch
and even my own breath
bears the wearing of wetness.

In this serene day
my heart slips easily
into the arms of peace,
content to be lost
in the love of receiving,

cherishing the heart of rain
as it sprinkles its moist grandeur
on the green forest before me.

I shall not fight for headiness.
I will be quite satisfied, instead,
to live in the lush stillness
that marks its truth upon my soul.

———————————

JOYCE RUPP

Childhood Memories
of Spring

Little did I dream when I grew up on a farm in northwest Iowa how much my experiences of the seasons as a child would help me love the seasons in my adult life. As I look back, there are many memories flavoring and influencing my awareness and appreciation of each season.

Springtime on the farm was filled with activity. Huge snowdrifts melted in the fields and farmyard making it a muddy mess for quite a while, especially if the spring rains were thick and frequent. Eventually the ground dried out and preparations for planting took place. Dad spent long hours from sunrise to sundown using the disk harrow or plow, readying the soil for the kernels of corn. In the garden, Mom was busy putting vegetable seeds in the ground and tending to her flowers.

On days when we were home from school, I was elated if I got to go out to the field where Dad was planting corn. I would walk out to where he was working and take his morning or afternoon snack to him. I'd spot him somewhere in the field and wave to him. When he came around with the planter to where I was standing, he would stop the tractor, find a shady spot on one side of it, sit down on the ground to rest, and eat his "lunch," as we called it then. This was usually a thermos of coffee, a sandwich or two with luncheon meat in it, and a cookie or something sweet. In the afternoons it was too hot for coffee, so Dad would lift the old crock jug wrapped with the remnants of a burlap bag. He would take big swigs of water from it while he ate his sandwiches.

Being there with Dad was a special moment. He worked hard, and I was glad he took a break to rest. I also loved being in the fields. When the rich, dark soil was turned over, I could see the patterned lines across the field that the planter made where the corn seed had been dropped in. I also liked to be there when Dad was disking the soil to cover up the corn, and smoothing out the field. It wouldn't be long and soon little green shoots would rise from that beautiful black earth.

One of my favorite childhood delights was when Dad brought home tiny bunnies he'd found after a rabbit's nest had been disrupted by his field work. Dad gave them to us to feed with our little doll bottles full of milk. The rabbits actually survived and grew, but then they mysteriously "got out" of the cage one night. I didn't realize until I was much older that Dad had let them go back out into the wild again.

It seemed like everything grew fast and strong in springtime. The clumps of purple irises in the grove were beautiful. The wild patches of asparagus in the ditches along our farm property were soon tall and ready for eating. Green growing things intrigued me and gave me a happy feeling. Working in the garden brought me satisfaction, whether it was seeding or weeding. I never put words on my sense of satisfaction then, but I think it was a child's discovery of how life could come from something so simple and plain as a seed. The amazing process of new life developing out of our hard work was an astounding revelation for me.

Spring was full of movement. Everything was birthing and growing rapidly. There were flocks of Canada geese flying north in the clear blue sky. Fluffy baby chicks peeped in the brooder house. Newly birthed pink pigs squealed in the barnyard. All sorts of insects and birds took up residence around the yard once spring was on its way.

This season also brought scary weather with it. I was deathly afraid of hailstorms, lightning, and tornadoes. Dad would go out in humid, unsettled weather and search the skies for signs of storms. He recognized hail clouds and would point them out to us, saying with a somber voice, "See that white one there by that big black cloud. There's hail in that one." I would shudder inside with fear when I heard him say that. He dreaded what hail could do to all those nice green, growing things in the field. I don't remember it, but Mom told me that when I was very small I was so afraid of bad weather that I would hide under the bedroom rug when I heard adults talking about possible storms coming our way.

Another significant part of my youth in springtime was the May Crowning event at our three-room country school. May was Mary's month for Catholics, and each year one girl was chosen to crown the statue of Mary. We had a procession of the school children, all decked out in our finest clothes, singing songs in honor of Mary. The girls wore wreaths of flowers in their hair. The white spirea bushes were usually blooming, so that's what we used for our wreaths. The fragrance was powerful and the white blooms, delicate. It was always a treat to be in that procession.

All these memories live on in me, and each spring I find myself energized by the fresh sun and greening earth. I always feel a need to drop a few seeds into the soil, no matter where I live. The urge to get my hands into the earth is strong. I yearn to live alongside the journey of seeds opening in moist earth, pushing fresh green up toward the sunlight. If there's no free earth space outside my dwelling, I get a flower pot or a planter in which to place the seeds. It doesn't really seem like it's spring until I've done so. Then I sit back with satisfaction and wait for the blessedness of rising green to reveal itself.

JOYCE RUPP

Resilient Tree

I was with you spring of '94
when the storm came
with its golden flashes
slicing open your body.
It was terrible!
And yet, a tinge of beauty
was present at the scene.
After the terrible beauty passed,
I lay my hand upon your broken body,
and wept.

Standing beside you
I kept vigil in silence,
mourning your destruction.
A bluebird came;
it sat in the heart of your brokenness.
Something in me lifted.

I was there spring of '95
when resurrection burst through
your brokenness, all green
and eager to begin again.
I stood amazed,
watching the daily process of life
emerging from your splintered soul.
 A healing, hidden balm
 seeped through your wounds,

bandaging you
in soft green garments.
The bluebird was there again,
circling round
and resting in your heart.

And now, the spring of '97
invites me to the window
to see you standing there again
adorned in new, green robes.

What is this mysterious life
that hides in brokenness
and then returns
a full grown song?

MACRINA WIEDERKEHR

Listening to Spring

How quietly the earth breathes forth new life.
How eagerly the sun bleeds forth the spring,

I am listening.

I am listening to seeds breaking open,
  to roots growing strong beneath the ground,
  to green shoots rising up from winter wombs.
I am listening to thorns blossoming,
  to barren branches laughing out new growth,
  to wildflowers dancing through the meadows.

*I am listening.**

I am listening to the forest filling up with song.
I am listening to the earth filling up with life.
I am listening to trees filling up with leaves.

I am listening.

I am listening to the sky with its many changing moods,
  to flashes of lightning, peals of thunder,
  to opening buds and greening grass.
I am listening to the breaking forth of light
in the vestibule of dawn.
I am listening to the freshness of the morning.

I am listening.

I am listening to the rain drops
  giving hope to thirsty gardens.
I am listening to the orchards
  pregnant with new life.
I am listening to the flowers
  bursting forth in rainbow colors.

I am listening.

I am listening to the brook,
     to the song of happy waters.
I am listening to music
     rising up from all the earth.
I am listening to spring
     soaring in on wings of life.
I am listening to the sounds of spring.

I am listening.

I am listening to prayers
     pouring forth from feathered throats.
I am listening to prayers
     rising up from misty waters.
I am listening to prayers
     of a meadow crowned with dawn.

I am listening.

I am listening to the growing
     in the garden of my heart.
I am listening to my heart
     singing songs of resurrection.
I am listening to the colors of life.

I am listening.

I am listening to winter
     handing over spring.
I am listening to the poetry of spring.

I am listening.

MACRINA WIEDERKEHR

*If this poem is used for a group service, an option is to have
participants echo after the leader the italicized *I am listening* that
follows each stanza.

The Blossoming Face of God:
A Spring Meditation

The awakening light all around us and our new awareness of the sacredness of creation reminds me of one of my favorite post-resurrection stories of Jesus and his disciples (John 21:1–14). It is that well loved story of the boys out fishing without any luck. They were fishing at night. As the light of dawn appears, a stranger on the shore quizzes them about their success in fishing. The stranger is Jesus, but they fail to recognize him. When Jesus tells them where to cast the net and they experience the great catch, the beloved disciple, John, suddenly knows the identity of this stranger. With joyful awareness he cries out, "It is the Lord!" The story ends with Jesus inviting them to gather around a charcoal fire on the shore and have breakfast. "Come and dine" is his invitation. It is significant that the disciples were fishing at night. The revelation comes at dawn, just as the light is returning.

This story reminds me of another unfolding revelation that is taking place in our world today. All around us the glory of God is breaking through creation's circle of life in the seasons of Earth each year. Yet, there are many for whom this Divine Face in creation remains a stranger.

Throughout the world prophets and lovers of creation are crying out like the beloved disciple, "It is the Holy One!" All this green! All this growing! All this light! It is the face of God blossoming through these branches. The Word of God is growing out of the land and shining from the skies. "Come and eat; feast at the table of Earth," these disciples keep inviting.

Through these new disciples, the Holy One keeps trying to tell us where to cast our nets. Unfortunately, there are still many seekers frantically searching for food to heal their weary spirits and wounded hearts who have not yet discovered this important medicine of the universe. At times they are even suspicious of these new disciples of the Word of God in creation. They gaze into this miraculous unfolding of life and do not see the face of God. The God of Creation remains as much a stranger to them as Jesus was to those apostles who were fishing at night.

The creative spirit of our Divine Artist, however, does not grow weary. Continually the voice invites, "Come and dine; feast at Earth's sacred table. Behold the Blossoming Face of God!"

Teardrops of Growth

April is soaking the world
with her spring tears.
They patter softly on the roof,
clinging to silent windows.
Gently they fall into soil
diligently turned
and ready for watering.

A touch of sorrow and joy
mingle in the wet spring air.
One part longs for sunshine,
the other accepts the patter
of April's mournful tears,

knowing this is what opens
hard shells of waiting seeds
and urges them to grow.

A patch of waiting soil in me
has also been turned over.
It, too, fights April teardrops
but knows it needs them
desperately.

So much in me has yet
to accept
the waters of discomfort
and discontent
that come without a beckoning,
urging me insistently to open up
and grow.

So much in me has yet
to be nurtured, broken open,
and set free.

JOYCE RUPP

Entering the Heart of Spring

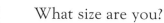

Begin by relaxing. Let your spirit rest . . . gently let go of busy things in your mind . . . allow your body to slow down. . . . Take a deep breath and let it out slowly. Do this three times. Gradually sink into a quiet place of ease and comfort.

I invite you to become a flower bulb. This might be a daffodil, an iris, a tulip, a hyacinth. . . . Choose one of your favorite spring perennial flowers and prepare to enter into the life of this flower. . . . Become the flower bulb.

What color are you?

Brown or gray, white or tan, perhaps a little pink or burgundy?

What is your shape?

Are you completely round, somewhat triangular, hourglass shaped?

What size are you?

A large bulb? Very small? A bulb with several others attached to it? Long? Wide or narrow?

What is the condition and texture of the interior and exterior?

Firm? Soft? Thin or thick skin?

Sit for a moment with the silence of the bulb.

Be with its stillness, its beauty, its potential for growth.

Now become aware of the loving hand of the Divine Gardener holding you, carrying you to a spacious garden. You feel safe in this hand, at home and at peace. You understand no harm will come to you. Outside the Divine Gardener kneels down on the ground. Soon you feel yourself being lifted with tenderness and placed into the ground. The Divine Gardener whispers to you: "Do not fear. You have a strong spirit. You must rest here for a while. In time you will experience a wonderful surprise."

Feel the soft earth welcoming you . . . breathe in the air that fills little spaces in the soil . . . sip in the moisture greeting your thirstiness. . . . Let your eyes adjust to the darkness. You know now that you have been placed in a womb where you will need to wait in faith for what is yet to come. . . .

Be with this womb of darkness. Wait in this place of gestation through the long months of late autumn and winter as the ground becomes frozen. What are the sensations you experience? . . . What thoughts go through your mind? . . . What longings are in your heart? . . .

Finally you begin to feel a little movement of the soil around you and a tiny bit of warmth. Then there is more warmth and some drops of moisture reach your dry throat. You realize how thirsty you have been. . . . You sense a stirring within you that continues to grow. . . . A burst of energy fills you and you feel yourself stretching . . . it's amazing . . . you feel new life emerging. . . .

You sense the energy within you. . . . You want to give all you have to this new shoot, to push it up, up, up above the soil . . . and now comes a sleek, shining, green shoot . . . alive! More juices and vitality from the soil energize you . . . the sun's warmth surrounds you and fills you with joy. . . . The more this happens, the more energy you have to send to the green shoot . . . and now this vibrancy from your heart is so strong in the green shoot that a bud begins to form . . . it is very small at first, undetectable. . . .

Then the bud slowly fills out. . . . All your strength moves into this bud and you see how she is beginning to open, quietly, surely. Ah, now you see it, a brand new bloom. . . .

Look at the color . . . smell the fragrance . . . enjoy her smiling presence as the soft wind moves her back and forth in the spring sunshine. . . . Lean back with ease in your bulb-ness and be grateful for the amazing birth that has happened through you. . . .

Hold the beauty of the blooming flower in your mind. . . . Hold the wonder in your heart. . . . Now, gradually come back to this time and place. . . .

Questions for individual reflection

1. What is the condition of your spiritual flower bulb?

2. Who or what has planted you in the rich soil of growth?

3. What helps you to wait with hope when growth is gestating in you?

4. What is now blooming in your life?

5. Can you sense anything that continues to be in the darkness, still awaiting birth? What might this be?

Integration

Draw your flower bulb and the bloom that comes forth from it.

Write a prayer or poem as if the flower bulb or bloom were writing it.

Go to your garden or to a flower shop and bring some spring flowers into your home. Place them in a vase and enjoy their story of growth and beauty.

A Spring Celebration

Place as many symbols of air as possible around the room (kites, balloons, incense, a child's soap-bubble jar, flute, etc.). Place feathers, one for each participant, in the center of a small table. Light four candles, one on each corner.

Song

Begin with a light-hearted song, one that sings of hope and joy.

Introduction

Spring is an energetic season of hope, a time of awakening, of stirring and coming alive. There is much movement happening everywhere. Windy days of March and softer breezes of April ride on the wings of spring, bringing energizing air and life-giving rains.

What a wonder and mystery air is! No one can see it, yet it contains what is necessary for life. As it circles the globe, it takes carbon dioxide to vegetation for nourishment and then carries oxygen for our lungs and blood back to us from the vegetation.

Air is permeable, expandable, difficult to contain. Like spring, air has a zesty freedom. It has immense energy and power. When air gathers speed, its winds clear out storms, smog, dust, and pollen. It bends strong trees and sends huge thunderclouds rolling over mountaintops. It sweeps rain across dirty streets and cleanses them.

For all its power, air is humble. We hardly notice it even though our body is wedded to this essential element each moment of our life. We easily take it for granted as our lungs breath in and out in a steady rhythm, gifting us with what we need to stay alive.

Meditation

 Let us pause to be attentive to our breath, to the air that is so vital for us. The mystic Hildegard of Bingen described herself as a feather on the breath of God. We join now in a breath meditation.

Breathing in: *I am a feather*

Breathing out: *on the divine breath.*

An alternative breath meditation could be:

Breathing in: "Spring!"

Breathing out: "Life!"

Take as much time as seems appropriate for this meditation, depending on the group's experience and readiness.

 ## Reading

So many things disguise themselves as hope. So much crosses our threshold, promising change or relief from present circumstances, that sometimes it becomes difficult to tell the difference between a reasonable hope and a misguided delusion. . . . Hope becomes easier to recognize when we learn that it rarely comes from outside us. More often it comes from within, emerging from the place where our deepest longings meet our willingness to make them real. In that place hope sheds its disguises, moving with grace and freedom to point us beyond our delusions toward the landscape of possibility (Jan Richardson, *Night Visions).*

Gathering Our Hopes and Dreams

Each person chooses a feather and takes an index card with a hole punched near the end of it, and a pipe-stem cleaner (chenille stem). Play light flute music as participants quietly reflect on this question: What is one of your unlived dreams, hopes, or longings?

Invite each one to select one hope or dream that he or she most wants to have come alive in their life. They write or draw this on the index card. Then tie the feather onto the pipe-stem and attach it to the index card.

Sharing Our Hopes

Form small groups and share the hopes on the index cards that are attached to the feathers.

A Commitment to Hope

Repeat after the leader, holding feathers in indicated position:

Hold feather up high.

I honor my hope and give it my best energy.

Hold feather out in front.

I keep my eyes on my hope and do not let it out of my sight.

Hold feather to the ear.

I listen to my hope and respect what it teaches me.

Hold feather down toward the ground or floor.

I stand strong in my hope and trust in its possibilities.

Hold feather to the heart.

I become one with my hope and cherish its presence.

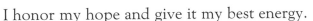

A Blessing of Hope (by leader)

May you give your hope room to breathe and expand.

May your anticipated dreams find a voice and a home in your life.

May hope move freely through your heart, gifting your spirit with enthusiasm and joy.

May you walk through spring storms with a strong sense of purpose, undaunted by fear.

May you never lose confidence in your ability to grow.

May your hope stream outward to the world, dancing in the far realms like a feather floating in an April breeze, bringing joy to all who need it.

Repeat each line after leader:

Spring, energizing spring.

Be our mentor of hope!

Spring, birth mother of greening, cheer us on!

Dance

All could dance freely to one of these songs or walk in a circle and sing:

"A Feather on the Breath of God" (Rosel Feder, *Mystic Suite*); "Do a New Song" (Julie Howard, *We Are the Circle*); "Wearing My Long Winged Feathers" (*Earth Dance Celebrates Songs of the Sacred Wheel*)

Conclusion

The ritual is concluded by going outdoors. Blow bubbles, fly kites, or let balloons sail in the breeze.

Carrying Spring in My Heart

This book provides a ritual for each season of the year based on the ancient custom of honoring the four directions of Earth. Similar symbols are used to represent the directions, but the text of the prayers for each season is different. The prayers are focused on each particular season. The following ritual celebrates spring. You will need these symbols: feather, candle, pitcher of water, a young green plant, bowl of soil, blossoms and/or green grass. Each of the prayers below can be prayed by various leaders or by the entire group.

East

Hold a feather and stretch up into the air with it, as though touching the stars and clouds. Move in a circle. Come back around and face east again.

Great Spirit of the East,

you are dreaming me,

singing me from the stars,

laughing in dawn's sunbeams,

calling me from little green leaves.

Dance your vision in my bones.

Birth your love in my being.

Surprise me with the taste of joy

and teach me the sounds of hope.

South

Begin with an unlit candle. Hold it near your heart to remember the winter that has just passed. Then, light the candle. Hold it *up high as you sway several times to the right and then to the left, dancing with the new light.*

Great Spirit of the South,

I lift up my face toward your light,

I unite my heart with your love.

Spring is promising me new life.

My fruitful times will be restored.

The emptiness of winter days

will be left far behind me.

Receive my gratitude.

Touch my open heart and fill it.

West

Take a pitcher full of water and pour a few drops of it gently upon a young green plant.

Great Spirit of the West,

even in springtime, surrender is required.

The yielding soil is broken open and readied

for the garden to receive the seed.

My springtime heart turns toward you

to receive the teachings you offer.

Give clarity to my decisions and actions

so I can release what keeps me from growing.

May every yielding of my strong will

be a graceful letting go so new life can stir.

North

Hold a bowl of soil with flower blossoms or stems of green grass lying on the top of the soil.

Great Spirit of the North,

light returns in abundance as spring appears.

Come with your strong rays of hope.

Come with your whispering winds of rain.

Send courage to accept the inevitable pain

that is a part of the birthing process.

May I lean into your strong embrace

as the first signs of revitalization

grow stronger in me every day.

A Celebration of the Spring Equinox

The ceremony begins with the group gathered around a large basket filled with packets of seeds. Some individual seeds are either strewn among the packets or are in a small bowl. Extinguish all light in the room. Invite the group to remember winter's darkness and dormancy. Recall the long months of the soil's stillness. After a time of silent sitting in the dark, welcome the light either with candles to fill the room with radiance or by turning on as many lights in the room as possible. If the sun is still brightly shining, the group could now go outdoors into the sunlight.

You will need: seed packets and also some individual seeds, a basket, a large planter or container of soil that is prepared and ready for planting, and a watering can with water in it or a small pitcher. You might also choose to have candles depending on whether the ritual occurs during the day or evening.

The word "equinox" comes from two Latin words, aequus (equal) and nox (night). In the calendar year, the equinox is the precise time when the sun crosses the equator. On this date, the length of day and night are closest to equal. The vernal, or spring, equinox usually occurs on March 21. This event of the sun marks the official beginning of springtime in the northern hemisphere.

Introduction

Today the sun crosses our planet's equator and gifts us with an equal amount of daylight and darkness. We continue to move from long nights of darkness into long days of light. We enter into springtime, the season when all that has been asleep in the loving arms of winter awakens. That which is dormant lifts its head upward toward the warmth of the sun. Today each seed smiles at the story of life held within its heart.

Song

The group now sings an alleluia or a chant that has a lively melody, e.g., "I Am Alive," from Out of the Ordinary by Joyce Rupp.

Blessing of a Seed

The leader invites each person to take an individual seed and hold it. After they have a seed, the leader continues:

Little seeds, you are seemingly inert and lifeless, but appearances are false, for you hold an immense surprise. You hold life! Within you are whiskered roots, thick green stems, and dancing leaves. All you need is a gentle hand to place you in the soil, the dazzling sun to smile on you with warmth, and the moist fingers of spring clouds to awaken you with raindrops.

The group is then invited to pause for a time to silently ponder the seed held in each one's hand. After this silent time, all hold out their open hand containing the seed.

O seeds, blessed seeds, you will soon be dwelling in the soil.

Grow, grow deep, grow strong!

Send your life forth into the sunlight.

We celebrate the secret of spring within you!

Hands are then lowered and the leader invites the group to hold the seed to their heart.

We, too, have the potential for greater growth hidden within us. The seeds of our hidden potential are waiting for us to encourage them to grow. Pause now to be aware of one seed of growth within you that is waiting to come to life . . . (allow several minutes for this).

Dialogue

Discuss in small groups or dyads(twos): What "waiting seed" in your life is yearning to grow?

(E.g., the seed of a talent or expertise, the seed of deeper spirituality, the seed of healing, the seed of a strengthened relationship, the seed of a new attitude.)

Planting

After the sharing, the group repeats the following after the leader:

O dormant seed within me,

I believe in your potential.

I will open the soil of my heart for you.

I will warm you with my patience and trust.

I will water you with droplets of faith, hope, and love.

All gather around the planter or container of soil. The leader invites each one to place a seed into the soil. After the seeds have been planted, each person takes the watering can (or small pitcher) and pours a few drops of water on the seeds.

Leader: We journey now out of winter and into spring.

Let us enter into the amazing power and vitality of springtime

with gratitude and awe.

All: Winter is past! Spring has come!

Great Miracle of greening and growth,

I turn my heart toward your light

as you resurrect my dormant gifts.

I turn my heart toward your warmth

as you draw me faithfully into fuller growth.

Circle around the planted seeds.

Close with "Dancing in the Spring."

Dancing in the Spring

Dancing, dancing, dancing in the spring (2x).

All together as we sing, let our gladness ring (2x).

(The dance movements: Form a circle, joining hands.)

Dancing *(move to the right one step)*.

Dancing *(move to the left one step)*.

Dancing in the spring *(move to the right one step and then to the left one step)*.

Repeat the above.

All together as we sing *(come into the center, drop hands on "sing" and clap hands).*

Let our gladness ring *(rejoin hands and come back out of the circle).*

All together as we sing, let our gladness ring (2x).

Dancing in the Spring

© Joyce Rupp

Summer

Season

of

Fruitfulness

Introduction to Summer

Summer is the season

when nature comes into its fullness.

ANGELES ARRIEN

Summer inherits spring's passionate urge for growth. Spring nurtures the seeds of new life, and summer energizes them. It is a season of fullness and productivity. The long days of summer's light encourage anything that has enough moisture to stretch its utmost toward the sun. In the early growth of spring, many shades and textures of green wake up smiling. As summer steals the show, the vegetation matures into a deeper green and grows thick and sturdy. Blossoms readily fill out into fruits and vegetables.

The abundance of produce signals the beauty and bounty of this rich period, for summer is the season of ripening and abundance. Thick fields of grain wave their green and golden stems. Farmers markets, verdant vineyards, productive gardens, lush flower beds, and fruit-laden orchards all give witness to the power of light and growth in this season.

Summer is the period of high temperature when solar rays are most directly focused on the planet. Intense energy accompanies these powerful waves of heat. When the sunlight is very strong it produces sweat, good old perspiration that rolls down our body on sweltering, hot days. Some avoid this heat by seeking air conditioned

113

places, but others simply accept the sweaty times as a part of summer's unique presence.

People, creatures, and the land are affected as temperatures rise. Each one's energy grows more sluggish with heat and humidity. Summer becomes a "lazy time" of sitting outdoors on lawn chairs and enjoying easy moments of relaxation. It is the season to gather around campfires telling stories, to watch fireflies at dusk, or to do nothing at all.

When the summer sun is too strong, it overwhelms growing things. Grass withers and garden plants quit producing. The land begs for water, yearning for relief from the unceasing heat. By early August, burnt edges of brown can be seen. In some parts of the country, the penetrating sun turns the land into a dry, straw-like desert.

In spite of the relentless sun, summer is a time of playfulness and leisure. It beckons us outdoors. There are lively sounds like the neighbor's lawnmower on an early Saturday morning, cheers at baseball games, and the pop and boom of firecrackers on the Fourth of July. If you listen, you can hear summer's hum in the locusts, crickets, tree toads, and cicadas. The songs of whippoorwills, cardinals, mockingbirds, robins, and loons on the lake reverberate everywhere. This hot season is evident in the splashing water of swimming pools, the voices of children at play in the park, and laughter at the zoo.

No matter where we live, summer brings a certain kind of freedom from care that is unlike any other time of the year. This season is full of playfulness. Imagine what summer would be like without vacations, time at the pool and the beach, barbecues, fishing and camping, biking and hiking, weddings and reunions, state and county fairs.

There are striking similarities between this season of fruitfulness and our inner life. Our interior summer is also full of light and growth. These two features are essential elements of our spiritual transformation, just as they are necessary for nature's growth and development. When we are "in the light" we are moved by an energy that assures us of our self-worth and our potential for growth. This assurance leads us into a period of energetic productivity where we develop our talents and gifts with enthusiasm. During this time, we are especially drawn toward activity that gives meaning to our life.

It is in our spiritual summer that we see glimpses of truth that have been hidden from us. Discoveries we would doubt or quickly pass by in another season are revealed and accepted. The light of our mind provides clarity and perception so we can more easily find direction for our journey. There is less confusion and hesitancy in our thought and decision making, fewer tensions and turmoil in our emotional space, more resonance between our inner and outer experiences.

During our inner summer, we know we are growing. There's a robust surge of spiritual vitality. We long to be faithful to our truest self. The desire to become more healed and whole grows stronger in us. During this time, we often sense the presence of divinity within ourselves and others. Sometimes an immense passion for the holy surges through our spirit. We feel as though we could give our all for deeper communion with this Beloved One, confident of a divine light within us that will never go out.

Life has less struggle when we are in our spirit's summer season. We are likely to experience playfulness and lightness of heart. An easy gratitude fills us because our work and relationships move along well. We feel productive and fulfilled as we recognize how we are contributing to the betterment of our world.

Our interior summertime moves us toward fullness and ripening. Perhaps reading a book helps us develop a fuller dimension of ourselves. A personal relationship might become stronger, enhancing our enthusiasm. Our summer growth could be a retreat or a seminar that nudges us toward something deeper and more vibrant. It might be an insight from our journal or our prayer that stretches us, or the learned practice of stopping to breathe once in a while so that we enjoy the now.

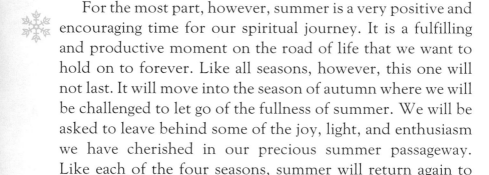

The shadow side of our spiritual summertime is that we can get overly involved in using our gifts and talents and begin to burn ourselves out just as the hot sun burns the green foliage and withers it. If our thrust into activity and productivity is not balanced with leisure and play, our productivity will soon limp and our ability to maintain high energy will dwindle and collapse.

For the most part, however, summer is a very positive and encouraging time for our spiritual journey. It is a fulfilling and productive moment on the road of life that we want to hold on to forever. Like all seasons, however, this one will not last. It will move into the season of autumn where we will be challenged to let go of the fullness of summer. We will be asked to leave behind some of the joy, light, and enthusiasm we have cherished in our precious summer passageway. Like each of the four seasons, summer will return again to our hearts when it is time, for every season's entrance and departure is part of the ever-turning circle of life.

Canticle After Vespers

(progressive view from a country porch swing)

Day is done

Three cows in the pond

One cow thinking about going into the pond

Fifteen cows grazing in the green shadowed grass

One cow mournfully mooing

      as though our world will never be healed

Three calves joyfully frolicking

      as though there is no need for mourning at all

Four layers of blue green hills as a backdrop

Three hummingbirds hovering over my head

Two mockingbirds sitting on the fence

One glowing sun descending in the west

One August moon rising in the east

Three lazy purple clouds saying their night prayers

Only God knows how many locusts singing from
the trees

A sweet summer breeze coming in from the east

One August moon growing larger

One lone firefly looking for a mate

One August moon growing bright as a harvest moon

Three stars coming out to look at the moon

One mooing cow (finally) lying down to rest

A great star family growing in number

The choir of locusts ending their song

Three more fireflies joining the loner

The canopy of night sky remembering the earth

A great silence falling upon me

A small joy spreading through me

A large wish for world peace washing over me

Fifty-five wordless prayers dwelling within me

Day is done.

MACRINA WIEDERKEHR

A Summer Prayer

···

May you breathe in the beauty of summer with its power of transformation.

May this beauty permeate all that feels un-beautiful in you.

> All: May the God of summer give us beauty.

May you seek and find spaces of repose during these summer months.

May these moments refresh and restore the tired places within you.

> All: May the God of summer give us rest.

May you be open to times of celebration and recreation that are so much a part of summer.

May you find happiness in these times of play and leisure.

> *All:* May the God of summer give us joy.

May your eyes see the wonders of summer's colors.

May these colors delight you and entice you into contemplation and joy.

> *All:* May the God of summer give us inner light.

May you feel the energy of summer rains penetrating thirsty gardens, golf courses, lawns, and farmlands.

May these rains remind you that your inner thirst needs quenching.

May your inner self be refreshed, restored, and renewed.

> *All*: May the God of summer give us what
> we need for healing.

 May you savor the fresh produce that comes to your table and enjoy the fruits of summer's bounty.

> *All*: May the God of summer give us a sense of
> satisfaction in the work of our hands.

May you find shelter when the stormy skies of summer threaten your safety.

> *All*: May the God of summer give us shelter when
> inner storms threaten our peace of mind and heart.

May you enjoy the unexpected and find surprises of beauty and happiness as you travel the roads on summer vacation.

> *All*: May the God of summer lead us to amazing
> discoveries as we travel the inner roads of our
> soul as well.

A Garden Reflection

··

Summer would not be summer for me without a garden, no matter how small it might be. The scents and sounds of a garden lure my soul into hope-filled mystery. I see miracles everywhere. The simplicity of a single seed presses into the soil and eventually transforms itself into a hearty vegetable. Blossoms on a cherry tree emerge as round embodiments of succulence. Grapes on a vine proceed to fill out their expanding skins. Ferns unfurl in the silence of the night. Flowers laugh themselves into kaleidoscopes of joy as they stretch toward the seducing sun. Green leaves wrapped in morning dew glisten, their colorful radiance sparkling before my eyes.

My spirit breathes in the mystery as I take in all the wonderment. It sighs with contentment. The garden's potential to nurture life is just what my heart needs. I gain inner strength from observing the garden's resilient and prolific abilities. I rejoice in the signs of growth before me, humbly acknowledging that I cannot force the garden to grow. I am only a caretaker for what is produced.

Without the intertwining of sun, rain, nutrients of soil, earthworms, bees, hummingbirds, and all of nature's essential helpers, the work of my hands and heart would be fruitless. With immense satisfaction, I look upon this process of growth, feeling called again and again to an undying truth: nothing is completely isolated and alone. Each part of life needs the other for its sustenance and well-being.

I work in the garden as a midwife: watering, mulching, weeding, pruning, and tending to its needs. As I do this, I resonate with the desire for life that sends a turnip's green stem pushing forcefully through thirsty soil in need of watering. I wince with pain for the strong button weeds as they are pulled out. I sympathize with the pumpkin vines that keep stretching beyond their boundaries, trying to take much more than their designated space. I whisper *thank you* to the freshly picked pea pods as they fill the garden basket. As my fingernails get dirty and my muscles feel the strain of caring for the garden, I know that the landscape of this nurtured haven is reflective of the landscape of my inner life. Without a doubt, my soul's growth needs a midwife's tending as well.

 Quiet communion with the garden revives the peace and tranquility that all too easily slip away from me. The garden's fragrances, colors, and shapes comfort my inner weariness. Its bounty feeds not only my body but also my soul. As I stoop, kneel, sit, and stand among the garden's verdant vegetation, I forget about the busy things that seemed so important to me.

In the garden I experience the restorative powers of nature. The garden becomes a sanctuary of repose and promise, a graced place that allows my body and spirit room to breathe freshness. In this restorative place hope feeds my discouragement. Faith feeds my doubt. Here in the garden I am reminded of my communion with all that lives.

Rise Early

Rise early
when summer darkness
still enwraps the trees.
Walk into the dark forest
with only your attentive heart.
Gaze toward the east,
take a deep breath, and wait.

After a short while you will see God
carrying a lantern through the forest,
bits of light bobbing up and down,
in and out, higher and higher,
the light climbs, spilling over
into the spaces between the leaves
and on into the world
beyond the forest.

Then the beautiful darkness
hands you over to the light.
It slips away reverently
into the bark of the tree trunks,
into the black earth,
into all those other countries
that wait for its return.

Lift your face to the daystar now.
Experience the coming of dawn.
Bathed in morning light, pray
that the lantern of your life
move gently this day
into all those places
where light is needed.

MACRINA WIEDERKEHR

Listening to Summer

Out of her pastel green pitcher
spring is pouring forth summer, and I am listening.
Out of her youthful, energetic body
summer is flowing, and I am listening.

*I am listening.**

I am listening to Earth leaning closer to the sun.
I am listening to the heat breathing through the
gardens,

>> drawing life out of seeds,

>> calling plants to fruition,

>> whispering fulfillment to the flowers.

I am listening to the growing circle of life.

I am listening.

I am listening to the ripening

>> in the orchards,

>> in the vineyards,

>> in the garden,

>> in the grain fields.

I am listening to the ripening in my heart.

I am listening.

I am listening to the summer of my soul,

to the dance of life within me,
    to the fruitful struggle of all that yearns for life,
    to the perspiration that sweats out toxic poisons.
I am listening to the warmth of summer.

I am listening.

I am listening to the song of the gardener
    bringing food to the table.
I am listening to the meadow's promise
    of winter hay for hungry cattle.
I am listening to Mother Earth
    growing wild with multiple vitamins.

I am listening.

I am listening to summer songs
    of leisure and renewal.
I am listening to the sound of happy voices
    playing on the beaches,
    shouting at the ball games,
    sharing stories on the porches.
I am listening to bare feet, laughter, and fishing poles,
    to summer picnics and mosquitoes.

I am listening.

I am listening to the spaces in between the green.
I am listening to young birds testing out their wings.
I am listening to morning filling up with sunlight.
I am listening to the music of evening twilight.

I am listening to the night chant of a thousand tiny
creatures.

I am listening.

I am listening to fruitfulness
    spilling forth from earth's rich womb.
I am listening to happy potatoes
    growing round beneath the ground.
I am listening to the green cathedral of the forest,
    to the stars that peep through summer branches.

I am listening.

I am listening to spring
    handing over summer.
I am listening to the poetry of summer.

I am listening.

—————————————

MACRINA WIEDERKEHR

*If this poem is used for a group service, an option is to have
participants echo after the leader the *italicized* I am listening
that follows each stanza.

Summer, a Season for Living

Today I've come out from behind my walls, away from my office. It is summer, and in spite of the heat I feel strangely happy. Instead of writing this in an air-conditioned office, I have chosen to be outside where summer's breath insists that I drink from the cup of reality. As I sit here in this large earth-sauna, in the shade of my favorite sycamore tree, I am suddenly aware of how I have distanced myself from nature. As I listen to summer's call, I discover that I have lost a part of myself behind walls. I have been housed too well. Walls have made me a stranger to the earth. My office sometimes makes me feel more important than I am, and I lose sight of essentials. One of those essentials is touching the earth. Summer invites me to plant my feet upon it again.

The best teachers to help us enjoy summer are little children. They do not yet work in offices. They do not own calendars with tasks crying out to be done. I love to see the parks fill up with young life each summer. The children's return to the earth is a good example for their elders. And so, when school is out, summer's children swarm the streets, parks, pools, lakes, and campsites. I am joining them for a day, lest I grow old before my time.

Under the sycamore tree, far away from my childhood summers, I am lost in reverie. It is not swimming pools and city parks that I remember. I see the creeks and forest swimming holes of long ago. These are some of the memories that speak to me of my childhood summers: bare feet in the creek bed, tadpoles and tiny fish swimming between my toes, the challenge of catching crawdads, watching for snakes, hanging from tree limbs, and jumping into refreshing pools of water. The forest and the meadow were my office. That's where I did my best work.

Some grownups tend to be obsessed with making a living rather than making a life. They become preoccupied with having a reason for doing whatever they do. Children need no reason. Life is the reason. Thus children can more easily live from the center, from the heart. It is a purer kind of living. It is living in the moment.

"Sacramental" is the word I would choose to describe my childhood summers. A sacramental is a tangible symbol that leads one into a sacred presence. As I continue my reflections on the gifts of summer, my memory goes back to some of those summer sacramentals.

I recall the "thump, thump, thump" of tapping on the watermelon trying to discern if it was ripe. In Forrest Carter's *Education of Little Tree*, there is a charming scene in which Little Tree's grandfather teaches him when a watermelon is ready to be plucked from the vine. Learning to listen to *sounds* is the key.

> You have to know what you are doing to thump test a watermelon and make any sense of. If you thump it and it sounds like a—*think*—it is total green; if it sounds—*thank*—it is green but is coming on; if it goes—*thunk*—then you have got you a ripe watermelon. . . . Grandpa thumped the watermelon. He thumped it hard. He didn't say anything, but I was watching his face close and he didn't shake his head, which was a good sign. It didn't mean the watermelon was ripe, but no head shake meant he hadn't given up on it. He thumped it again. I told Grandpa it sounded might near like a *thunk* to me. He set back on his heels and studied it a little more. I did too. . . . He said as near as he could tell, it was a

borderline case. He said the sound was somewheres between a *thank* and a *thunk*. I said it sounded like that to me too, but it 'peared to lean pretty heavy toward the *thunk*.

That story brought back memories of my own summer living and listening to the watermelons. After the ripest one was selected, I remember that earthy, sacred moment of eating the melon. Outside under a tree we sank our faces into that red-green world of sweetness. The earth was our table. It was a far cry from a seven course meal where you have to keep one hand in your lap.

The feel of my bare feet in the grass is another happy memory. Today I can scarcely believe I darted through the tall grasses without a thought about snakes and ticks and chiggers. I think Earth heard me coming and rejoiced at the thought of me walking on her sacred body. "This is my body," she proclaimed, "and you are a part of the soil of my soul." I didn't hear her voice back then. I didn't need to hear it because I had not yet distanced myself from her. I was obedient to an inner call. Today our sacred Earth is having a greater challenge in getting us to hear her voice.

At night there were a thousand little things singing from the trees. The night sounds of the locusts delighted me and lulled me to sleep. "Resurrection bugs," we children called them. We would find the shells they had shed hanging on trees. We decided that somewhere along the way they climbed out of them like Jesus coming out of the tomb. That's why they were singing. It was their Easter cry. This was our childhood theology. Forget about being politically correct. We gathered mounds of "resurrection shells" during those wonderful summers. Thankfully they have all returned to the soil.

Those were the days when I prayed summer without knowing it was a prayer. This was sacramental living at its best. All those liturgical processions through the fields and forests enriched me. With my whole being I was proclaiming the gospel of daily life.

What I miss most from those childhood summers are the porches. They were like outdoor chapels where the family was brought together. Porches were places where, on lucky summer nights, breezes passed through. There were stories, songs, and games. We took turns on the porch swing. What the world needs now is a place with more porches, a world where people do not have to be afraid to sit on them.

How easily the seasons speak to me of God! Yet, as I sit here underneath my sycamore tree experiencing the heat and longing for rain, I realize I do not have the same fondness for summer that I had as a child. My childhood summer memories do not even include a thought of heat. I simply do not remember being hot. I was so involved in life I did not have time to notice the discomfort. Summer was a celebration of life. It was the time I lived most intensely, holding nothing back. It was the season of total commitment to life. I joyfully participated in the sacrament of summer because I was still in the process of receiving the sacrament of childhood. As a child I was quite successful at living life fully because I had not yet learned to live by the calendar. I lived by heart.

MACRINA WIEDERKEHR

Praying With the Gospel of Summer

1. If you want to be attentive to the prayer of summer, ask for help from the child who lives inside you. Every age you've lived through still resides in your soul, thus help is never far away. Ask the child within to help you remember how to live by heart. If you cannot find the child within, any child will do. Ask a child for help.

- What are some childhood memories that suggest you once knew how to live by heart?
- Share some of these memories with someone you enjoy.
- Make plans to go for a walk with a child. (Luke 10:21–24)

2. The elements of creation offer excellent material for summer prayer. Go outside and look around. What colors and sounds of life do you see? Use the growing season outside to help you pray with the growing season inside yourself.

- What kind of growth is taking place in the country of your heart?
- Make a promise to yourself that some day soon you will spend a whole day in a green place.

3. May your commitment to spiritual growth be as obvious as the wonders that take place in your backyard. David Hays, a mountain hermit and poet, said it like this:

When heat comes to the mountains even the flowers go mad.

They get hasty in the yard pushing colors at each other

and reaching for the sun that drives the seed.

- Have you ever felt this kind of passion for spiritual growth?

O Antiphons for Summer

O BREATH OF SUMMER,
Come! Come with your warm winds.
Breathe on all within us that resists growth.
Temper our desire to be in control.
Raise up some wildness in us.
O Come!

O FIREFLIES OF BEAUTIFUL EVENINGS,
Come! Come enchant us with your mystic dance.
Brighten our evening with your little lights.
Lead us away from day's duties.
Lift our spirits into your carefree flight.
O Come!

O GARDENS OF PLENTY,
Come! Come bless us with your wealth.
Sustain us with your abundance.
Remind us of the world's hunger.
Nudge us to give from our fullness.
O Come!

O DAZZLING SUN,
Come! Come with your golden rays.
Anoint us with your energizing beams.
Recharge us with your radiant vitality.

Refresh our overworked spirits.
O Come!

O Festivals, Fireworks, Feasts, and Fairs,
Come! Come with barbecues, crafts, and games.
Unite us in the common bond of our desire for joy.
Entertain us with the simple things of life.
Deepen our gratitude for all things good.
O Come!

O Long Days of Extended Light,
Come! Come with your wide expansive arms.
Open our eyes to the daily miracle of life.
Slip into our distracted hearts with every dawn.
Expand our ability to see beauty in our world.
O Come!

O Summer Word of God,
Come! Come with your transforming breath.
Breathe on us until we are ripe with life.
Fire us to be light for the world.
Nourish us with your healing rays.
O Come!

O Source of Growth and Light,
Come! Come encourage us to stretch toward light.
Warm us with your abiding presence.
Challenge our lethargic spirits.
Walk with us into the deep, green forests.
O Come!

Summer Stars

A quiet sense of oneness
ripens in me as I gaze
into evening's summer sky.

I behold this endless space
filled with sparkling lights,
speaking of a world unknown,
luring my heart into mystery.

Dancer of the Stars,
I am at home with you
when I view these galaxies
of ageless beauty.

Without a breath of help from me
the heavens display their splendor.
Their twinkle and glow sparks joy,
igniting hope in my humbled heart.

When I doubt your presence
I need only step into the night
and behold the stars beyond me.
One look assures me of presence.
One gaze enwraps me with awe.

Playmate of the Pleiades,
as you roam amid the stars
beauty settles in my soul,
and peace comes drifting in
with the gift of gentle greeting.

JOYCE RUPP

August Rain

Rain this morning,
all morning long
and well into the afternoon,
August rain,
slow, steady drops of water,
holy water,
interspersed with mini storms,
streams of lightning,
darting passionately
into the weary soil.
The humid,
oppressive August heat flees.
I breathe more easily.
I smile.

Sometimes
my thoughts,
like August heat,
hang heavy and smothering,
creating an oppressive,
unfriendly climate.
Then suddenly,
some holy spirit, falling
as rain upon my desolate land,
descends like a blessing,
some sweet spirit full of hope

washes away the heaviness,

lightening up those hostile thoughts

till they are filled with loving kindness,

falling on those around me

like a rain of grace.

MACRINA WIEDERKEHR

Childhood Memories of Summer

Summer was a wonderful season. The long evenings of light were special times in my childhood. When supper was over and chores were done, we children were free to stay outside till dark, playing all sorts of games that held us in laughter and simple fun. We cavorted around energetically playing *Hide and Seek, Annie-Annie Over, Red Rover,* and *Statue.*

Those happy times of playing until dusk are why early evening is still my favorite time of day. I loved the long, long evenings of light. The night dew on our bare feet was cool as we ran on the expansive lawn. The birds twittered for one last time before putting their heads under their wings for the night. The fireflies we caught and placed in our jars glowed mysteriously. There was a large screech owl living near one of the walnut trees. My older brother often succeeded in terrifying me by telling me that the owl was going to get me as it flew over us at nightfall. It didn't keep me from loving the time after supper, though. That playful time was always a magical moment for me.

Before my sister Lois and I were old enough to have lots of chores on the farm, we spent many daylight hours out in the grove playing "house" under the trees. We didn't get in much trouble except for going into the chicken house and getting real eggs to use in our mud-pies. One year Mom cleaned out an old, small building called a "brooder house" that was used for hatching little chicks. She let Lois and me have it as our playhouse. We thought we were in heaven when we had a real house all to ourselves.

Then, there was Saturday night in the summer. My parents left us eight children alone when my oldest brother was in his early teens so Mom and Dad could have a night in town, getting groceries and visiting friends. They didn't know what kind of dangerous antics we kids pulled while they were gone. We went down to the cattle-yard and swam in the huge water troughs used by the cattle. We jumped in the corn bins filled with grain and sneaked over to the neighbor's place (because their folks were in town with our folks) where the oldest boys practiced rifle shooting and we younger ones played games. By the time my folks got home we were all snug in bed just as we were supposed to be. They never found out about the corn bin, not even when my sister had a kernel of corn stuck in her ear one summer, but they did discover the rifle practice which quickly put an end to that adventure!

As I grew older I constantly helped outdoors. I loved being with the land, gardening, planting and helping in the fields, baling hay and bringing in the golden oats of summer. Mom made jams and jellies out of ripe elderberries and chokecherries that we picked in the grove. I even enjoyed weeding and mowing the lawn. Anything to get me outside with the land and the animals.

One of the few jobs I hated was "walking the corn," which meant walking down rows of corn in every field in order to pull out the weeds. It was a hot, sticky job in humid Iowa air. If the corn was very high, and you were very short, the sharp edges of the corn leaves could slice your arms and face if you were not careful. Being short of stature, I often had a lot of "corn scratches." Between the pollen, the sharp leaves, and the bugs, I detested that job and couldn't wait for us to get finished with it.

One year when I was in eighth grade, I was allowed to make some money by raising cucumbers to sell. "This will be a cinch," I thought, not realizing that the only cucumbers most farm wives wanted were tiny ones about as big as my little finger. They used these to make sweet pickles, which meant many hours for me of back breaking picking from the prickly cucumber vines. I sold bushels and bushels of those tiny green things. After that summer was over, I never wanted to see another little cucumber again.

My memories of summer are mostly filled with inviting images, however. The smell of the newly mown alfalfa field was perfume to me. The star-studded sky at night was an orgy for the eyes. I could lie for hours gazing at the beauty of the heavens. The sky had an immense clarity on the farm where no city lights took away the glimmer of the vivid constellations.

My mother taught me how to garden. I never realized until I moved away from home how unusual it was to have so much of our own fresh food. It was always a treat when the first cantaloupe ripened, when we had our first meal of sweet corn, and when the red, juicy tomatoes were ready to be eaten.

There are many summer memories that I treasure. Certainly one of the best is the vacation we each took every year at our cousin's farm. Dorothy and Ed were childless at the time we were growing up. Each of us children got to take a few days by ourselves to spend with them. We never had to do any work, got to have some of our favorite foods, and were treated as royal guests. It was the time to be "an only child," and this wonderful couple loved us as their own. One of the sad things about growing up was that my summers no longer included a vacation of my own at Ed and Dorothy's farm.

Because of so many cherished childhood memories, summer continues to draw me to the expansive outdoors. I find myself feeling cheated when it rains too much in summer, or I have too much work to do to allow me to spend time outdoors. For it is there, amid the early chirps of robins at dawn and the first twinkle of fireflies at dusk, that I am energized and filled with contentment.

JOYCE RUPP

A Summer Blessing

Blessed are you, summer,
season of long days and short nights,
you pour forth light from your golden orb,
energizing the earth and calling forth growth.

Blessed are you, summer,
with your generous gift of heat.
Your warm breath animates creation,
encouraging all growing things to stretch toward the
sun.

Blessed are you, summer,
you call us into playfulness,
encouraging us to pause from work.
You renew our spirits.

Blessed are you, gracious season of summer,
you surprise us with a variety of gifts from the earth.
We, too, gaze into the earth of ourselves,
beholding gifts waiting to be honored.

Blessed are you, nurturing season of summer,
your fruits and vegetables appear on our tables,
changing them into altars.
Tasting of your life, we are made strong.

Blessed are you, summer,
host of a star that shines with passion.
Sun-soaked, we reach for your energy
that drives us upward and onward.

Blessed are you, sacrament of summer,
nature's green season, sweet echo of spring.
You speak to us in living color as you renew the earth
with symbols of life for our bodies and souls.

Blessed are you, summer,
season of roots that reach for water.
Even through the cracks in the sidewalk
the song of your seed can be heard.

Blessed are you, summer,
season rooted in reality.
Even as the perspiration collects on our brow,
we experience your earthy joy.

Blessed are you, summer,
with your firefly evenings
you minister to the child in us.
You feed our hunger for beauty.

Getting Up on a Summer Morning

I am never quite ready
to begin the day
until I see the night angel
blowing out the stars,
the angel of dawn
rolling in the golden bowl,
or the cloud angel
laughing down the raindrops.

Throwing on the cloak of dawn
my sleepy summer heart
forgets its craving for comfort,
remembering a deeper hunger and
I am up and out to taste the weather
whatever it might be:
hot and humid,
warm and sunny,
rainy, stormy,
maybe even the gracious gift
of a summer breeze.

As the day grows I, too, grow
lighthearted, attentive, free,
patient, grateful, wise.
Healed of indifference,
I fall in love once more.
There is something about
embracing the day
with the intimacy of a lover
that makes one well again.

Only one thing is necessary,
a heart with a single eye.
My desire for spiritual healing
must be fierce. I must decide
to breathe myself alive
in any kind of weather.

The tools are given
and I decide.

MACRINA WIEDERKEHR

A Proclamation of the Power of Fire

We proclaim that the lights of the cosmos unite all people on the planet in a great oneness. As the fiery stars, the intense sun and the reflective moonlight shine on us, so they bathe each one who dwells on this beautiful sphere of life with a great illuminating energy.

We proclaim that there is an unquenchable fire shining within each person, a light that is strong, deep, and enduring. It is the vigilant fire in the hearth of the soul, maintaining hope and truth amid life's many ups and downs.

We proclaim that the fire of those who have gone before us has never left this earth. We are heartened by the truth that their sacred fire has become an eternal light that leads us on, a fire continually blessing us, encouraging us, affirming us to live our life to the fullest for our own benefit as well as for the good of all humankind.

We proclaim that the fire within cannot be contained. It seeks to move out, to permeate, to enter into every place that lacks passion and vitality. When the inmost self is opened with love, trust, and confidence, an energizing and healing light shines forth to fill the corners of the world.

We proclaim that there is a divine fire within us that is immeasurably loving, inconceivably caring, consistently nonjudgmental, and enormously passionate. This light will never give up on us. It will cherish us into eternity.

We proclaim that the light within us is beautiful, precious, and wild. We urge everyone to do all they can to tend this fire, to care for it with courage and kindness. Let the inner light shine forth radiantly so all will benefit from the power of this immense warmth and goodness.

Entering the
Heart of Summer

Begin by relaxing. Let your spirit rest. . . . Gently let go of busy things in your mind. . . . Allow your body to slow down. . . . Take a deep breath and let it out slowly. Do this three times. . . . Gradually sink into a quiet place of ease and comfort.

Place yourself on a country road. It is a warm summer day. The sun is hot and you feel its strong rays. . . . The air is thick with humidity. . . . There's not a cloud in the deep blue sky. . . . You look for shade and see there is a small farm nearby. . . . You walk toward the farm where there is a small pond in the field. . . . There's a large garden plot near the house . . . and an orchard beyond the garden. . . .

Go to the garden. . . . Walk around it. Notice the various kinds of vegetables it contains. . . . Look at the colors . . . the shapes . . . the sizes. . . .

Find one vegetable in particular that has grown and is ready to be taken from the garden, maybe lettuce or a tomato or some green beans. . . . Stand near this vegetable. . . . Lean down and touch it. What does it feel like? . . . What color is it? . . . Does it have a particular odor? . . . Let the vegetable tell you about its ripening process, how it feels to be strong and full, to be at the peak of growth. . . .

Move on slowly, walking beyond the garden to the orchard. . . . Feel the comfort of the shade that the trees provide for you as you walk among them. . . . Find a tree that is filled with ripened fruit. Sit down beneath this tree and rest in the shade. . . .

Look up at the tree full of fruit. . . . Stretch out your hand and pick one piece of fruit from a low hanging branch. . . .

Hold it in your hand and see how beautiful it is. . . . Then take a big bite from it. . . . Taste the juice and the flavor. . . . Roll it around in your mouth and savor it. . . . Swallow it with great satisfaction and contentment. . . .

Continue slowly to eat the fruit, tasting it as fully as possible. Enjoy this moment of pleasure in the summer orchard. . . .

You rise up now and stretch, looking up at the tree and thanking it for the gift of the delicious fruit you've just eaten. . . .

You begin to walk out of the orchard . . . back past the vegetable garden . . . out to the place where you began. . . . As you do so, you feel again the power of the sun warming your body. . . . Notice how your feet feel as you walk on land that can produce such wonderful life-giving things. . . . Now you reach the place from which you started this journey. Turn around and look at where you have been. . . . Ask to remember the loveliness of this summer moment. . . . Now slowly return to this time and place.

Questions for Internal Reflection

1. What vegetable did you find? What did you notice? Does it have any significance for you?

2. Do you find any connection between its story of ripening and your own journey of growth?

3. What kind of fruit was on your tree in the orchard? Does it reflect some part of your life?

4. Who and what brings you joy and a sense of satisfaction?

5. Where in your life do you feel fruitful, completed, at peace?

6. What part of your life do you recognize as still ripening, still being readied to be shared?

Integration

Take a vegetable or a piece of fruit. Sit and hold it in your hand. Don't do anything. Just be with this ripened produce for at least five minutes. Enjoy the beauty you hold in your hand.

Write a dialogue between you and the fruit you have chosen. Ask it to tell you about its journey to fruitfulness.

Go for a walk. Offer a quiet litany of thanks for all the things in your life that seem fruitful now.

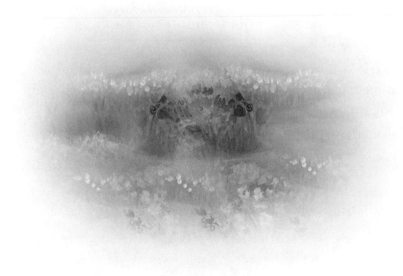

Dancing Flame: Celebrating Our Inner Fire

....

One large candle burns on a table. All participants are given a transparent bowl containing a small candle.

Introduction

Summer is the season of light. Generous amounts of sunshine fall from the heavens. That touch of fire invites all growing things to leap into fullness. The steady flame of the sun ignites a passion in the land, and everywhere we are able to behold the dancing flame of life. As you witness this exuberant and fruitful unfolding in the earth, you are encouraged to turn your gaze to your inner life. Call down the sacred fire from the heavens to greet the fire in your soul.

We ask you now to remember your dreams and visions, your hopes and passions: all those lights that you thought had gone out. Call them home. Hold them close!

This is the night of the Great Rekindling.

Rekindling

A moment of silence

There are many stories in religious traditions of people celebrating the sacred flame of their lives. One that readily comes to mind is the rekindling of fire found in the beautiful Easter Vigil. The fire in the sanctuary that has burned before the blessed sacrament all year has been put out. A new fire outside the church is lit and blessed. The new fire is then carried into the church.

The people follow the new fire in procession. All receive a light from the Easter Candle. This service is a celebration of light burning through the darkness and a remembrance of the Hebrew people being freed from tyranny and oppression.

In this service we acknowledge that our inner fire often grows dim. The fire of our faith, hope, and love weaken and need to be rekindled. There is always a spark within, waiting for us, a spark that has not completely gone out. As we gather in prayer we want to honor and feed that little spark. We invite the great lights of heaven and earth to nourish and bless our own hidden fires, the fires that have grown dim.

All lights are now turned off and the large candle is now extinguished. The leader reads the following short meditation in which participants are asked symbolically to receive the great fires of the heavens and the earth, and to invite those fires to rekindle and nourish their own inner fires.

Here in the darkness we remember the great lights of Heaven and Earth:

O Fire of the bright burning daystar, O sun,

Fire of the soft glowing moon,

Fire of the twinkling stars,

Fire of the brilliant planets,

Fire of the galaxies,

Fire in the earth,

Fire of hope that shines on in the midst of violence,

Fire of love that flames up even in the hearts of those who have been wronged,

Fire of forgiveness that rises up out of the ashes,

Fire of faith shining through the eyes of the dying,

Fire of wisdom radiating from elderly faces,

Fire of compassionate presence bringing joy to the lonely.

The memory of these lights helps us remember our own inner fires that darkness can never put out. We invite these fires to rekindle and encourage our own wavering flame.

After a few moments of silence the leader asks the participants to echo these words:

May the sacred fires of Heaven and Earth
rekindle the fire in each of us.

The large candle is now lit.

Prayer Over the New Fire

Be for us

a sacred fire—sanctifying us

a fire of compassion—warming us

a fire of forgiveness—healing us

a fire of purification—cleansing us

a fire of creativity—inspiring us

a fire of justice—summoning us

a fire of love—rekindling us

a fire of change—healing us

a fire of passion—empowering us

a fire of the Divine—illuminating us

O Fire of God, transform us.

Burn away all hardness of heart.

Free, O set free the fire within us.

Break down the walls we have built.

Let your fire leap through our resistance

over the walls of our hearts

and out into a world yearning for transformation.

Burn into our hearts these words of Jesus,

"I have come to light a fire on the earth;

how I wish the blaze were ignited!" (Luke 12:49).

After a few moments of silence listen to the song "Transforming Fire," Melodies of the Universe by Jan Novotka.

Sharing

Have participants share in dyads: What fire in me needs to be rekindled? What is the kind of fire I long to bring into my world?

Dancing Flame

After the sharing, leaders get light from the new fire and light the candles of seven or eight people. When the first group has received their light, one by one they stand, raise their bowl of light, and proclaim their gift of fire for the world's healing. They are now invited to move in a free form circling dance around the table carrying their bowl of light. (You may wish to use a chant for the circling dance or it may be done in silence.) This same process continues until each group of seven or eight has received the fire, proclaimed their gift, and circled the table with their bowls of light.

154

After the last group has circled the table invite them to mingle with one another, exchanging their bowl of light with another and greeting them with a peace wish (e.g., Sister [Brother] of Light, Shine on!).

A Proclamation of Fire

Close with the entry, "A Proclamation of the Power of Fire" (p. 146).

Carrying Summer
in My Heart

·····························

That this book provides a ritual for each season of the year based on the ancient custom of honoring the four directions of Earth. Similar symbols are used to represent the directions, but the text of the prayers for each season is different. The prayers are focused on each particular season. The following ritual celebrates summer. You will need these symbols: feather, candle, pitcher of water, a bunch of grapes, and a vase flowers. Each of the prayers below can be prayed by various leaders or by the entire group.

East

Recall a hope or dream of yours. Hold feathers near a part of your body to symbolize this hope or dream, e.g., near the head for clear thinking, the heart for faithful loving. . . . An alternative movement would be to do smudging. The burning of incense in certain religions is done in order to purify an area used for ritual and to designate the sacredness of the spiritual actions taking place. Smudging bears some similarity to this. It is a spiritual practice used by Native Americans and other native peoples. It consists of burning sacred herbs, such as sweet grass, cedar, sage, or tobacco, and using the smoke to cleanse or purify the body, the ritual area, an object, etc. The smoke is directed with the hands, or with a feather, over the person or the thing one wishes to smudge. If smudging is used, it should always be done respectfully and reverently.

Great Spirit of the East,
sunrise smiles in my heart.
Morning rejoices in my bones.
Your love cleanses my worn ways
with the power of resurrection.
Bring forth my hidden creativity.
Let it rise with gifts to be given.
Speak to the secret places within
and draw me into your wildness.

South

Light a candle. Take the grapes and hold them up. Eat several of them slowly and enjoy the plentiful gifts of summer.

Great Spirit of the South,
giver of abundant fruitfulness,
restorer of passion and enthusiasm,
I gather the richness of summer
with its contagious aliveness.
Your colors, strong and full, astound me,
like grapes inside me ripening on the vine.
I gather baskets of fruitfulness
and celebrate the wonders of growth.
Thank you for your overflowing goodness.

West

Have the water in a wine goblet or chalice. Drink from it as a gesture of gratitude for receiving the fullness of summer and for being willing to let go of this fullness when it is time to do so.

Great Spirit of the West,

I enter into sunset with peacefulness.

It is the season of generosity,

time to receive, time to give.

The sun shares long days of light and energy

and night comes with welcoming rest.

Turn me toward your beckoning call.

I open the full hands of my heart

and pour out the graciousness of your love

upon all who dance within the cosmos.

North

*A vase of flowers. Take a flower, smell it, kiss it, place in your
hair or behind your ear.*

Great Spirit of the North,

your summer breath is sweet and warm,

saturating the flowers with perfume,

chasing the stars with moonbeams.

You bid me partake of Earth's beauty.

It stirs in my soul and sings in my prayer.

I stand with a sense of satisfaction,

keenly aware of this season's bounty.

Good memories of this summer feast

will flow through me for many long winters.

A Celebration of the
Summer Solstice

··

olstice is taken from two Latin words, sol, sun, and stitium, to stand still. The summer solstice is the time of year when the sun is at its greatest distance from the equator, a time when it appears that the sun has stopped moving higher in the sky. On this day the length of time with sunlight is the longest. The summer solstice is usually celebrated on June 21 in the northern hemisphere and on December 21 in the southern hemisphere.

The group sits in a circle around an unlit bonfire or a cluster of unlit candles. The leader welcomes the group, facilitates introductions, and invites them to reflect on what summer means to them. After a time of quiet, each one shares her or his central experience of the season of summer.

Song

Following the sharing, all join in a song such as: "Awakening to the Radiance" (Coming Home, Kathy Sherman), "Infinite Sun" (Earth Dance Celebrates), "Where I Sit is Holy" (Bread for the Journey, Shaina Noll), "Circle of Life" (Gift of God, Marty Haugen).

Introduction

The leader announces the celebration of the summer solstice:

Summer is the season of the radiant sun, of succulent fruits, long days, short nights, dancing flowers, fireflies, steamy weather, and radiating heat. It is the season when the warm intensity of our sun signals vegetation to leap into fullness. The steady flames of the sun ignite a passion in the land, urging the fertility of all living things to produce an abundance. On this summer solstice we gather to celebrate the day of longest light, this season of potency when the fiery rays of our immense sun fill our hemisphere with intense heat and energy for growth. Let us rejoice in the power of the sun and its ability to give life to our planet. Let us also rejoice and celebrate the inner light that sustains us, the light that empowers our spiritual ability to grow deeper and stronger.

The group stands and raises their arms, extending them upward toward the sun, repeating each line of the following after the leader:

Sun! Radiant Sun!

Great gift of the Creator of Light!

We claim the passion in our bones!

We embrace the fire in our soul!

O fertile hopes and dreams awaken!

Let us rejoice in this longest day of light!

Sun! Radiant Sun!

Reading

The group is seated and a reader describes how the Celtic festival of Beltane is connected with light:

The festival of Beltane was an ancient Celtic celebration of early summer. At this time, fires in the cottage hearths were extinguished. This was very significant because the fire was vital as the source of heat, cooking, and light. A new fire was started on the highest hills where huge bonfires were lit. The people would carry the light from these fires from one hill to another, until all the high hills had great fires burning. After much dancing, singing, mirth-making, and celebration, they would carry the new fire home to their hearths to be kept burning until another Beltane. The passing of this physical light was a powerful symbol of the rebirth of vitality, energy, hope, and the rekindling of dreams. The fire was a symbol of the fertility of the land and the people. It was a celebration of the embers of life coming into full flame again in the season of summer. The fullness of the sun and the dancing flames of the fires on the hillsides re-lit the passion for life within the people.

Lighting of the Fire

A bonfire or the cluster of candles is now lit. All walk around the fire in a clockwise direction three times. This is done in silence while they ponder the flames, the light, the warmth. Then, the refrain of whatever song used previously is sung again. Following this, the leader invites those present to reflect on their inner fire, their passion for life.

Reflection

The questions below can be printed so each one can reflect on them, or the leader can read the questions to the group and allow some time for the group to consider their response.

What is your life's passion at this point in your journey?

Is it still hidden or has it made itself known to you?

Is it waiting in the wings?

Is it alive and active?

How would you name it?

How do you feel about it?

Are you living it?

What is your approach to it?

Has it influenced your own and others' lives?

What do you need in order to have the flame in your soul leap with life?

Dialogue

Form small groups of five or six. Each is invited to share what their life's passion is.

Conclusion

After the sharing is completed, the group stands in a circle around the fire. Each one calls a word or phrase that names his or her inner fire or passion. When this is completed, the group once more moves in a circle around the fire three times, singing the song chosen above, or some other song with a theme of light, passion, and vitality.

Autumn

Season

of

Surrender

Introduction to Autumn

Delicious autumn!

My very soul is wedded to it, and if I were a bird

I would fly about the earth seeking successive autumns.

GEORGE ELLIOT

As the hemisphere of the planet slowly continues to tilt away from the sun, the season of autumn comes on stage. Autumn has a distinctive change of personality from spring and summer. This is the season that has often been associated with melancholy. Its mood is mysterious and nostalgic. The reason autumn is often called fall is not necessarily because leaves fall from trees. This is the season when Earth slowly falls away from the sun and light rays are lessening. This lost light, of course, will spring back to us in six months. The amount of sunlight reaching Earth's surface determines the kind of changes that take place each season.

Autumn is a royal season. To temper the necessary disrobing of the glory of summer, autumn dons a coat of many colors, for beauty softens departure. Autumn holds fragments of the other seasons in transformative arms. Even while forecasting an end to lush green summer, we are still gifted with some warm, green moments. The quiet turning of the leaves from summer green to radiant arrays of color offers us a splendor as lovely as the blossoms of spring. Sitting in autumn's quiet sunlight can be a sonnet without words. Ever so slowly, this season turns its face toward winter. It is a bridge between the warmth and the cold. Beginning with summer's dew still in its hair, it can quickly become a friend of winter's frost.

Everywhere there are icons of autumn. In their spectacular flying formation the geese honk their farewells as they begin their journey to warmer lands. With great drama the squirrels scurry about filling their winter cupboards with nuts and acorns. Animal coats thicken in preparation for winter. Groaning cornstalks become musical instruments, swaying and whistling as the wind moves in and out of their crumbling bodies. Blackbirds swish through the sky in great numbers. Leaves dance in the wind and blow across yards as though they are walking on water. Children, and adults with childlike hearts, roll in the leaves laughing happily. Sometimes they lie quietly in the leaves in a dreaming state while experiencing a sacred connection to the earth.

It is harvest time. A sense of completion and accomplishment enwraps the land. Earth invites us to gather the fruits of her womb. From soil and vine, from tree and bush she pours out food to humankind and to creatures of the land. Fields of grain send forth their blessing. Trees laden with fruit sing sweet songs of nourishment. Vines thick with pumpkins display their beautiful readiness. Grapes and tomatoes generously offer their gifts. Potatoes and peanuts buried in the earth reveal their maturity. In the midst of all this harvesting, how appropriate that we should pause from our labors to celebrate a festival of gratitude: Thanksgiving. Earth is our table. Gratitude turns over in our hearts during the fall season, like an old-fashioned plow turning the soil.

The mood of autumn is the ebb and flow of life. Autumn stands as an epiphany to the truth that all things are passing and even in the passing there is beauty. It holds out platters of death and life. As the bright colors of fall fade away, and the leaves make their final descent, rich brown and charcoal colors take center stage. This is a decaying season, but the rotting ritual that surrounds us has another face. Compost and mulch are food for the soil. There is life in the dying. Moments of death are full of life and our fear of the unknown sometimes hides that life. All this dying is a prophecy of life to come. Everything is dying to live.

While many people dread the approaching winter season, often these same people claim autumn as their favorite season. Perhaps this says something about the haunting call of this season to turn our eyes toward home. Autumn touches the core of the soul with its wordless message about the necessity of transformation and death. We are gently encouraged to look toward the west and embrace the bittersweet truth that all things are transitory. As we face the painful reality that nothing lasts forever, autumn teaches us humility. We learn to honor the dying. Everything is moving, flowing on into something new.

In this lovely season when the dance of surrender is obvious, we find large spaces left where something beautiful once lived. As one by one the leaves let go, a precious emptiness appears in the trees. The naked beauty of the branches can be seen, the birds' abandoned nests become visible. The new spaces of emptiness reveal mountain ridges. At night if you stand beneath a tree and gaze upward, stars now peer through the branches. This is an important autumn lesson—when certain things fall away, there are other things that can be seen more clearly.

This same truth can be celebrated in our personal lives. When we are able to let go of a relationship that is not healthy, the heart is given more room to grow. We are able to receive new people into our lives whose gifts we never noticed. These people come to us with their own visions and dreams. If we are receptive, our lives are enriched. Perhaps it is not a person we have lost, but a dream of good health that would last forever. Our health fails; our dream dies. People often speak of becoming more grateful after having lost some of their health. Suddenly they see all they have taken for granted. Gratitude for all that has been enables them to say yes to all that is to come.

Another significant area of surrender comes with possessions. Our possessions can become little gods that eventually get in our way. Yet, it can be very difficult for us to turn things loose that have ceased to give us joy. When the wondrous moment of letting go of something that is not serving our spiritual life arrives, however, a unique and joyful freedom is born.

There are those who struggle to discover the blessing and wisdom of the aging process. The surrender of youth can be most difficult of all. To these I would say, "Sit for a while with a young tree; then plant yourself in the shade of an old tree. Let these share their wisdom."

Autumn is a wondrous metaphor for the transformation that takes place in the human heart each season. When we notice a subtle change of light outside our windows, we know the dark season is near. Everything is being prepared for winter. Autumn calls us in from summer's playground and asks significant questions about our own harvest: What do we need to gather into our spiritual barns? What in our lives needs to fall away like autumn leaves so another life waiting in the wings can have its turn to live?

It is easy to read the human story in these autumn pages between summer and winter. This is the season that evokes nostalgia and pours longing into human hearts. Autumn speaks of connection and yearning, wisdom and aging, transformation and surrender, emerging shadows, and most of all, mystery. This is the season that touches our longing for home, for completion. We are invited to let go, to yield . . . yes, to die. We are encouraged to let things move in our lives. Let them flow on into some new life form just as the earth is modeling these changes for us.

The season of autumn will not stay with us forever. It will fall into the womb of winter. In this dark resting place another dimension of growth will reveal itself. Each season's entrance and departure is part of the gracious turning of the circle of life. Autumn will return to the land and to our lives when it is time. The wheel keeps turning.

Falling Leaves

O falling leaves of autumn,
what mysteries of death
you proclaim
to my unwilling self

what eternal truths
you disturb
in the webbings
of my protected heart

what wildness
you evoke
in the gusty dance
of emptying winds

what mellow tenderness
you bravely breathe
in your required surrender

what challenge
you engender
through your painful twists
and turnings

what howl of homelessness
you shriek
with your exile of departure

what daring task
you evoke
as you feed the hungry soil.

O falling leaves of autumn,
with each stem
that breaks,
with each layer of perishing,

you teach me
what is required,
if I am to grow
before I die.

JOYCE RUPP

Listening to Autumn

Autumn is slipping through summer's branches
    and I am listening.
I am listening to the dying
    flowing forth from autumn's being.
I am listening to the life
    hidden in the dying.

I am listening.*

I am listening to the trees taking off their lush green garments.
I am listening to the leaves turning, turning, ever turning.
I am listening to the burning bush of autumn.
I am listening to the falling of this season.

I am listening.

I am listening to the song of transformation,
    to the wisdom of the season,
    to the losses and the grieving,
    to the turning loose and letting go.
I am listening to the surrender of autumn.

I am listening.

I am listening to the music of the forest's undergrowth,
    to the crunch of leaves beneath my feet,

to the miracle of crumbling leaves becoming earth
again.

I am listening to the beauty and fragility of aging.

I am listening..

I am listening to the wheel of the year turning,

to the cycle of the seasons,

to the call for harmony and balance.

I am listening to the circle of life.

I am listening.

I am listening to days growing shorter,

to the air turning crisp and cool,

to the slow waning of the light,

to the stars that shine in cold, dark nights.

I am listening to the growing harvest moon.

I am listening.

I am listening to happy harvest cries,

to hearts overflowing with thanksgiving,

to tables laden with gifts from the earth,

to baskets overflowing with fruit,

I am listening to the bountiful gift of autumn.

I am listening.

I am listening to a call for inner growth,

to my need to let go of material possessions,

to my need to reach out for invisible gifts.

I am listening to a call for transformation.

I am listening.

I am listening to the death of old ways.
I am listening to the life force turning inward.
I am listening to the renewal of the earth.

I am listening.

I am listening to summer
handing over autumn.
I am listening to the poetry of autumn.

I am listening.

MACRINA WIEDERKEHR

*If this poem is used for a group service, an option is to have participants echo after the leader the italicized *I am listening* that follows each stanza.

Prayer of Acceptance

The summer ends, and it is time

To face another way.

WENDELL BERRY

Eternal One who circles the seasons with ease, teach me about Earth's natural cycle of turning from one season to another. Remind me often of how she opens herself to the dying and rising rotations, the coming and the going of each of the four seasons. Open me today to the teachings of the season of autumn.

When I accept only the beautiful and reject the tattered, torn parts of who I am, when I treat things that are falling apart as my enemies,

> walk me among the dying leaves, let them tell
> me about their power to energize Earth's soil
> by their decomposition and their formation of
> enriching humus.

When I fear the loss of my youthfulness and refuse to accept the reality of aging,

> turn my face to the brilliant colors of autumn
> trees, open my spirit to the mellow resonance
> of autumn sunsets and the beauty of the
> changing land.

When I refuse to wait with the mystery of the unknown, when I struggle to keep control rather than to let life evolve,

wrap me in the darkening days of autumn and
encourage me to wait patiently for clarity and
vision as I live with uncertainty and insecurity.

*When I grow tired of using my own harvest of gifts to benefit
others,*

take me to the autumn fields where Earth
shares the bounty of summer and allows her
lands to surrender their abundance.

*When I resist efforts to warm a relationship that has been
damaged by my coldness,*

let me feel the first hard freeze of autumn's
breath and see the death it brings to greening,
growing things.

*When I neglect to care for myself and become totally absorbed in
life's hurried pace,*

give me courage to slow down as I see how
Earth slows down and allows her soil to rest
in silent, fallow space.

*When I fight the changes of unwanted, unsought events and
struggle to keep things just as they are instead of letting go,*

place me on the wings of traveling birds flying
south, willing to leave their nests of comfort as
they journey to another destination.

*When I fail to say "thank you" and see only what is not, instead
of what is,*

lead me to gather all the big and little aspects
of my life that have blessed me with comfort,
hope, love, inner healing, strength, and
courage.

Maker of the Seasons, thank you for all that autumn teaches
me. Change my focus so that I see not only what I am leaving
behind, but also the harvest and the plenitude that my life
holds. May my heart grow freer and my life more peaceful
as I resonate with, and respond to, the many teachings this
season offers to me.

An Autumn Teaching

As I drove the long distance home for Thanksgiving, I studied the country fields with their rolling hills of rust, brown, and gold. They were completely barren, having recently been stripped by harvesters. Patterns of curving hills, flat terraces, and empty corn rows caught my eye and held my heart. I thought of how Earth nurtures, produces, energizes, and gives herself to the process of creating an abundant crop all through the spring and summer months. She welcomes the rains, endures the dryness, embraces the strong winds, receives the hot sun, and accepts the weeding that is needed for her seeds to grow and mature.

Then autumn comes and with it the gobbling mouths of combines, eager to gather the plentiful grains. The huge machines roll through the fields at a steady pace, chopping down, lifting up, husking off, tossing in, and taking away all that Earth has worked so hard to produce through the active months of growth.

There are two ways to view all of this, I thought, as I drove along the autumn scene. One is to see the land stripped of riches, summer fullness ripped from the soil in which the seeds were planted. Another is to see the land as a generous giver, offering what was produced, yielding a harvest to the reaper, gracious in giving of ripened grains ready for picking.

The latter view stayed with me and nestled comfortably in my mind. Earth seemed ready to be at rest after intense months of growth. I saw how she was prepared to accept future fallowness, and I imagined her at ease, grateful to be unworked, peacefully approaching her winter repose. With this approach, I saw how she receives for herself after she has given her harvest away. Earth becomes the one to accrue what she needs, leaning back and breathing easily in order to restore her depleted energy, welcoming the blankets of snow that protect and nourish her emptied soil. I noticed how Earth is equally generous in her abundant giving and in her emptied state of receiving.

As I reflected on how Earth graciously yields and moves from the season of harvest into her winter mode of emptiness, I recognized how much she has to teach me about being content to wait, to linger, to hibernate, to relish inactivity through my own empty seasons. I thought about my busy life and wondered why I had not learned and lived this wise lesson. I questioned my aversion to letting go of my productivity, giving away, being emptied, and waiting for restoration.

Questions arose. Why did I think I could ignore my need to recoup my energies? What caused me to fight my emptiness and non-productivity? What would help me lean into going slower, being quieter, resting and relaxing, instead of trying to produce one harvest after another without giving my inner land a rest? When would I realize how essential it was to restore and recover my inner resources? Why did I fight this natural process so much?

That long drive home for Thanksgiving was a turning point in my busy life. Earth gave me a significant teaching with her autumn voice. It is one that has stayed with me and has continued to influence how I live through the inner seasons of my life today.

A Litany of Water*

We are children of the waters. . . . Our planet is enveloped by a permeable yet fragile cloud of moisture that sustains life and renews those who dwell on this earthly home.

SAMUEL TOVEND

Water of the seas, vast and deep,
regenerating essence of our planet's vigor.

Water of the rivers, creeks, and flowing streams,
strong carriers of life, steady currents of movement.

Water of aquifers and irrigation systems,
soothing arid lands, nourishing hungry seeds.

Water of human tears,
cleansing drops of grief, dancing drops of joy.

Water of baptismal fonts,
inviting humanity into the circle of community.

Water of secret springs and ancient holy places,
providing sources of healing and transformation.

Water of raindrops and snowflakes,
caressing the land with needed moisture.

Water of wells, springs, and reservoirs,
life-giving dwellings of health and vitality.

Water of clouds, vapors, mists, and fog,
numinous vessels of wetness and silent mystery.

Water of the human body,
purifying, transporting, energizing, restoring.

Water of the womb, cradling precious life,
vital wetness recycled from oceans and sky.

Water! Water! Wonderful Water!

*Some indigenous groups associate the element of water with the direction of the west, the place of sunset and transition. These qualities are inherent in autumn.

An Autumn Blessing

Blessed are you, autumn,
chalice of transformation,
you lift a cup of death to our lips
and we taste new life.

Blessed are you, autumn,
season of the heart's yearning,
you usher us into places of mystery
and, like the leaves, we fall trustingly
into eternal, unseen hands.

Blessed are you, autumn,
with your flair for drama
you call to the poet in our hearts,
"return to the earth, become good soil;
wait for new seeds."

Blessed are you, autumn,
you turn our faces toward the west.
Prayerfully reflecting on life's transitory nature
we sense all things moving toward life-giving death.

Blessed are you, autumn,
you draw us away from summer's hot breath.
As your air becomes frosty and cool
you lead us to inner reflection.

Blessed are you, autumn,
season of so much bounty.
You invite us to imitate your generosity
in giving freely from the goodness of our lives,
holding nothing back.

Blessed are you, autumn,
your harvesting time has come.
As we gather your riches into our barns,
reveal to us our own inner riches
waiting to be harvested.

Blessed are you, autumn,
season of surrender,
you teach us the wisdom of letting go
as you draw us into new ways of living.

Blessed are you, autumn,
season of unpredictability.
You inspire us to be flexible
to learn from our shifting moods.

Blessed are you, autumn,
feast of thanksgiving.
You change our hearts into fountains of gratitude
as we receive your gracious gifts.

A Closer Look at Thanksgiving

If you sit on the bank of a river,
you see only a small part of its surface.
And yet, the water before your eyes
is proof of unknowable depths.

ANITA DIAMANT, *The Red Tent*

If you look at a sunset, you might see only the disappearance of daylight.

If you look beneath, you may see darkness opening the splendor of stars.

If you look at illness and disease, you might see only physical diminishment.

If you look beneath, you may see it as a teacher bringing you vital wisdom.

If you look at a broken relationship, you might see only a harsh ending.

If you look beneath, you may see the courageous seeds of new growth.

If you look at lost dreams, you might see only disappointment and doubt.

If you look beneath, you may see the stuff that new dreams contain.

If you look at the death of a loved one, you might see only pervasive sorrow.

If you look beneath, you may see that love lives on forever in the heart.

If you look at the planet's pain and creatures' woe, you might see only despair.

If you look beneath, you may see hope woven in the compassionate care of many.

If you look at yourself, you might see only tarnished unfinishedness.

If you look beneath, you may see your basic goodness shining there.

If you look for the divine being, you might see mostly unresolved questions.

If you look beneath, you may be astounded at the availability of divine love.

Thanksgiving is a time to look beneath our external lives for the unwavering love, the ceaseless peace, and the enduring strength that lie in the deep waters of our soul. The more we trust the "unknowable depths" of our existence, the more the power of gratitude becomes a song we daily sing. With what do you struggle today? What might lie beneath that struggle for which you can give thanks?

JOYCE RUPP

Autumn, a Season for Transformation

utumn, my favorite season, is a mystical time with a beautiful language all its own, a language my soul understands, no translation needed. A kind of eternal longing wells up in me that seems stronger in autumn than it does in other seasons. Perhaps it is my own forgotten memories of a source of life behind the life I now know, my own unrealized yearnings to return *home*.

I love to walk in the autumn woods. I feel as though I am walking in a womb of mystery. All around me life is changing, moving on into new forms and shapes, dying that it may live again. All that is falling away motivates me to see more deeply the unique mystery that I am. The many changes in the world of nature are symbolic of changes happening in human hearts. Autumn, with its unforgettable face of both acceptance and surrender, ushers in the *sacrament of absence*. This absence can be a blessing. My life becomes cluttered with many things. This is the season that invites me to let go. Sometimes what is not visible enables me to see new horizons.

I often hear people talk about spring cleaning, which involves anything from going through closets and downsizing to cleaning the house from top to bottom. I personally like to use the season of autumn to do this. It fits well with the house cleaning that nature is doing. For the past few years, it has become my custom in autumn to evaluate what needs to be relinquished in my life. Sometimes possessions weigh me down. At other times it is my character flaws that burden not only me but everyone who lives with me as well. I look into my closet and my heart each autumn and ask, "Is there anything I could surrender that would help me become a freer person?"

One of the things I enjoy about autumn is that, unlike myself, it looks like it's having fun surrendering. There is a playfulness about it. All those bright colors and falling leaves! As a child I used to stand in the midst of dancing leaves on a windy autumn day. My face turned upward, my hands stretched out, I would gather the leaves in my arms like birds falling from the sky. On some days I would try to keep my eye on a single leaf, following it wherever it led me, which was sometimes over the fence into the neighbor's pasture. One day, having worn myself out, my mother found me asleep in a big pile of leaves. The memory is a good one and I find myself wishing I would wear myself out playing a bit more in my adult years.

The season of autumn portrays the beautiful art of surrender. This festival of dying often stirs up emotions of grief in me. I recall that this favorite season of mine as a child was also edged in sadness. Autumn was butchering time. That was the part of autumn I didn't like. I hated to see the animals die even though I now realize that all of this is part of the circle of life. Autumn, indeed, is a time of surrender. The animals surrender their lives, the fields, vines, and trees hand over their grains, nuts, and fruits. The hardwood trees let go of their leaves. Flowers die and grasses wither. Even the animals have to let go of their secret hiding places as the meadows are mowed for hay.

When I was a child I, too, had a secret place, a little hideaway, a refuge where I would go when I wanted to be alone. I remember autumn as the season when even my secret place was stripped away. My hiding place was in the cornfield, underneath the stalks and long slender green leaves, but I knew that by mid-September the cornfield would be a secret place only for the field mice. Everything was harvested as grain and fodder for the animals: stalk, husk, grain, and cob. There were no secrets left at all. It was one bedraggled plot of land looking much like a battlefield. Of course, if I peruse all this in a more positive way, I could say the materials that once fashioned my secret place were transformed into food for the animals.

Autumn leads the seasons in modeling the sacred practice of recycling. What seems to die bespeaks a quiet truth; that which falls into the earth is never lost. The earth receives it and preserves it. Thus it becomes a nurturing source for new beginnings as another cycle of growth arises. This miracle of transformation is autumn's prayer.

In my ministry I become acutely aware of the spiritual autumns that move through the lives of the people I serve. Constantly they experience the death of letting go that has emerged out of their autumn-like surrenders. At times their lives seem to be one great litany of falling leaves:

- Parents letting go of their children, entrusting them into Hands greater than their own.

- The death of relationships, the confusion, anger, sadness, loneliness, and guilt, the agonizing over what went wrong and wondering if anything can be restored.

- The surrender of addictive ways of living, the pain of trying to loosen one's grip on the old way and live in a new way.

- Letting go of that youthful look in a society that tries to keep everyone looking young, questioning whether there is any wisdom to offer others in the aging autumn years.

- Letting go of old patterns of thinking that cripple and imprison us in narrow, lifeless places.

- Relinquishing good health, the many doctors' appointments, the medicine, the chemo treatments, the pain and fear of slowing down.

- And finally, the great falling leaf of *death*.

As I listen to this litany of falling leaves in autumn's vespers hour, I seem to hear my own voice asking, "How can I give shade with so much gone?" At moments such as these, I like to remember the seed that sleeps in the ground of my being, the compost of my life that, when invited, can rise up and bless me.

Sometimes when we are left empty with serving, it is a signal for us to start taking care of ourselves in healthy ways. This season of harvest and transformation is a good time to look for ways to nurture our homesick spirits. One way to bring about this nurturing is an exercise that I call "A Harvest of Memories."

When the cool weather leads us to light our furnace's pilot light, we can take a little time to attend the pilot light of our heart. Autumn is a good season to recall some of the fallen leaves of past memories. Bring out old picture albums. Gain new life and energy by remembering people who were once sheltering trees, places where we went for shade and refreshment. Their leaves may have fallen, but we can still live in the shade of their memories.

MACRINA WIEDERKEHR

Praying With the Gospel of Autumn

························

The passages that follow are for your autumn prayer. They are sacred writings from the Christian gospels and from the mystical poems of the Bengali poet Rabindranath Tagore (1861-1941).

1. Read John 12:24

   Jesus suggests the dying of the seed is a necessary dying so that new life may arise. In the spiritual autumns of your life, what have some of your necessary deaths been?

2. Rabindranath Tagore is a much loved poet of India. (1861-1941) Reflect on his poem taken from Show Yourself to My Soul, translated by James Talarovic.

   When death comes to your door
     at the end of day,

       what treasures

         will you turn over to him?

   I'll bring
     my full soul before him.

   I'll not send him away empty-handed
     the day he comes to my door.

Into my life-vessel

    pours the nectar

        of countless evenings and dawns,

            of numberless autumn and spring
                nights.

My heart gets filled

    with the sight of endless fruits and flowers,

      with the touch

        of joy and sorrow's light and shade.

All the treasures I've gathered

  during my lifelong preparation

    I'm now arranging for the last day

      to give it all to death—

        the day he comes to my door.

In relation to your daily deaths, have you ever offered such a sweet welcome as depicted in Tagore's poem above? Take special note that death is not treated as an enemy here but rather as a guest with whom you will share the treasures of your life. } *death*

3. To continue your autumn prayer, list some of the people in whose shade you once lived. Let this be a harvest of memories.

O Antiphons for Autumn

O SEASON FULL OF REMEMBERING,
Come! Come with your golden shawl.
Come scattering the beauty of well-aged leaves.
Strengthen us for changing our old patterns.
Give us memories that sustain our dreams.
O Come!

O COOLING BREATH OF AUTUMN,
Come! Come with your natural paradox.
Show us our fullness and emptiness.
Breathe into us a spirit of gracious acceptance.
Tame our desire to have summer stay forever.
O Come!

O SEEDS SPRUNG LOOSE FROM DYING PLANTS,
Come! Come teach us to be generative.
Carry us to places where we can take root.
Encourage the seed of our love to fall freely.
Gift us with the grace of surrender.
O Come!

O HARVESTER OF WISDOM,
Come! Come fill us with the waters of wisdom.
Show us the beauty of aging with grace.
Prepare us for the long, dark nights.
Gather from our lives all that has potential.
O Come!

O GLEANER OF GARDENS AND FIELDS,
Come! Come gather what is most precious in us.
Urge us to embrace our cornucopia of goodness.
Stir up gratitude and a sense of wonder.
Move us to give freely of our abundant harvest.
O Come!

O RUSTLING LEAVES FALLING FROM THE TREES,
Come! Come live inside our aching goodbyes.
Teach us the truth of life's impermanence.
Empty us of all that does not bless others.
Draw us into the waiting soil of wintertime.
O Come!

O RISING HARVEST MOON,
Come! Come dance your beauty into our world.
Carve a path of light between night shadows.
Soften our transitions with your moonbeams.
Shine on all weary travelers of the heart.
O Come!

O FIRST WHITE FINGERS OF DEADENING FROST,
Come! Come with your touch of mortality.
Carry us into the heart of deepest truth.
Befriend that which needs to die in us.
Teach us to be ready for the great letting go.
O Come!

Gratitude

· · · · · · · · · · · · · · · · · · · ·

To be grateful for what is,
instead of underscoring what is not.

To find good amid the unwanted aspects of life,
without denying the presence of the unwanted.

To focus on beauty in the little things of life,
as well as being deliberate about the great beauties
of art, literature, music, and nature.

To be present to one's own small space of life,
while stretching to the wide world beyond it.

To find something to laugh about in every day,
even when there seems nothing to laugh about.

To search for and to see the good in others,
rather than remembering their faults and weaknesses.

To be thankful for each loving deed done by another,
no matter how insignificant it might appear.

To taste life to the fullest,
and not take any part of it for granted.

To seek to forgive others for their wrongdoings,
even immense ones, and to put the past behind.

To find ways to reach out and help the disenfranchised,
while also preserving their dignity and self-worth.

To be as loving and caring as possible,
in a culture that consistently challenges these virtues.

To remember to say or send "thank you"
for whatever comes as a gift from another.

To be at peace
with what cannot be changed.

JOYCE RUPP

Childhood Memories of Autumn

As an adult I have struggled in the past with autumn's arrival. I have fought the reminders of death and letting go that autumn tends to bring because I did not want summer to end. I have clutched onto summer's light and fullness with a tenacious grasp and complained mightily when the end of the season came. Autumn was a huge interruption and brought with it the challenge to let go of the playfulness and leisure of warm, sunny days.

My attitude toward autumn has grown much more positive in recent years, but it still does not measure up to how I lived with autumn when I was young. As a child, I recall no struggle with summer's ending. Autumn was a time equally as wonderful as summer. I entered into the season naturally, savoring the fragrance of falling leaves and harvested fields. I accepted the cooling of the air and the darkness that gathered more fully every day. It never occurred to me that I ought to move back into summer. Autumn called to me and I went running into her arms with easy abandon.

The first strong frost was always a parting moment from the greening of summer to the browning of autumn. This sharp cold snap changed things significantly. It separated one season from the other. I liked the first frost. There was an energizing chill in the air and even though vegetation was soon wilted and lifeless, it meant that now the harvesting would begin in earnest. Memories of harvesting may not exist for those whose childhood was lived in cities, unless they had a rather large garden, but for those of us who lived in rural areas, harvest was the centerpiece of autumn.

One of the things I most remember about this season on our Iowa farm was the harvesting of the many fields of corn. How I delighted in seeing the wagons heaped high with golden kernels of grain. It was a great hurrah for all the hard work of planting and tending the fields. I would often go down to the granary where Dad, or my older brother, was unloading the wagon. Bushels and bushels of corn clinked into the auger shaft taking it up to the open door into the granary. They worked long into the night. The sun would set, the chill of autumn's air would settle, the moon would rise, and still the wagons full of golden kernels came into the farmyard. A spirit of abundance and happy satisfaction settled in my heart each year as this pattern of harvesting repeated itself. I never tired of it.

A friend of mine from Wyoming told me that as a child her strongest harvesting memory was not that of golden corn but of wagons and wagons of potatoes. She spent long hours with her family in their hundreds of acres of potatoes, shaking the dirt from the vines and making sure that every potato, no matter how small, was hoisted into the wagon. As she described this harvest scene of over fifty years ago, she said she could still smell the soil on the potatoes. Despite the immensely hard work she endured, my friend assured me that it was also a very satisfying experience for her.

Like my Wyoming friend, everything on our Iowa farm that we had planted and nurtured with our hard work in the garden and the fields was taken from the land in autumn. The pumpkin and squash vines dried up with the first hard frost. Soon after, these vegetables would be brought in to the food cellar and stored for winter.

Flowers, too, eventually lost their glow and green. When they changed to a dry, rustling brown we would pick seeds like cosmos and zinnia and save them for next spring's flower beds. I liked the scratchy, dry feel of those seeds in my hands. They looked drab and worthless, though, not sturdy and solid like a kernel of corn or a bean seed. Pausing to look at them, I often marveled at how they could hold a future flower inside of them.

Everything that grew during the summer was liberating its seeds in autumn. This generative nature of plants to produce seeds to carry on their lineage before they died also astounded me. Many of these small vessels of potential life either fell naturally to the ground or were carried away by wind and birds during autumn. The tattered weeds along the creek, the grasses by the fence line near the grove, the milkweeds facing the road, each one had some sort of seed they prepared and gave away to earth in the fall.

As autumn days progressed, the land grew more and more barren. Leaves fell from the tall cottonwoods and the young maples into deep layers on the expansive lawn. Many a day my siblings and I raked the leaves and rolled in piles of them, not minding at all the dusty, buggy condition, until finally one day we had to take them all to the burning pile. We would wait until evening when the wind settled before lighting the pyre of leaves. As we went into the house for supper, the smell of burning leaves would float through the air and follow us in the door. I never minded this at all as a child. The odor of those leaves as they ascended into the autumn air is a comforting seasonal fragrance forever stored in my memory.

In spite of the developing barrenness of the land and trees, there were significant scenes of beauty: the vertical and horizontal patterns of the oats stubble and the emptied rows of corn after all the grain had been gathered, the harvest moon rising in the east, especially when it was round and full, the feathery frost when it caught green plants and painted them with white frosting, and the deeper layered look of the stars at night as darkness came ever earlier. All of these sights caught my heart and wed me to autumn's beauty.

One of autumn's sounds that lifted my heart, and does so even to this day, was the constant gathering of flocks of birds as they joined company to head south for the winter. I often heard a flock of noisy blackbirds before I saw them filling a tree as they paused for a rest. I especially loved the v-formation of geese honking their way over the farm. I would watch their journey in the sky until I could only see specks on the horizon.

My autumn memories as a child have deepened in me as I have grown older. They draw me into a season that engenders gratitude for both the material and spiritual harvests of a year gone by. It is a season rich with wisdom, reminding me time and again to treasure the beauty, appreciate what is, and then, let go when it is time.

JOYCE RUPP

A Well of Wisdom

Guided Visualization

Each of us has a well of wisdom from which to drink. Each of us has an individual source that waits for us to discover it and draw from it in order to fill our thirsting spirits. This does not mean we are to disregard the wisdom contained in the wells of others. Rather, it is an encouragement to trust our own resources, to believe that what is held within our own well is also of immense value and worth. Too often we are led to believe that the wisdom of someone else's well is better than ours. We can so easily treasure their wisdom and discount the marvelous source of spiritual and intellectual nourishment within ourselves.

Our wisdom is often hidden in a very deep source. Reflection and silence are essential in order to find it. We are continually called to go within to discover this precious jewel. Let's pause now as I lead you to your inner well of wisdom, the well that is waiting to nourish and refresh you.

Close your eyes. Breathe deeply three times and each time let your breath out as slowly as possible. Relax your body . . . ease your mind . . . let your emotions be still. . . .

Sink into a quiet place and let yourself be at peace. . . .

Imagine now that you are looking through a window into your inmost being. There is a well within you . . . go to find this well . . . take your time . . . you will find it. . . . This well might be a small flowing stream, or a quiet pool, or a bubbling mountain creek, or a hidden spring . . . or it may be a deep well such as one finds on a farm or a ranch. . . . Be quiet now as you search for your well. When you find your well, sit down beside it.

Now take a look at your well's location.

Is it near a well-kept garden, in an open field, hidden deep in a forest, in a desert . . . ? Is there anything else around your well . . . a stone, a tree or a tree branch, a person, animal?

Dip into your well and taste the water . . . make a cup of your hand and lift the water to your mouth . . . feel it flowing through you, refreshing and renewing you . . . let the power of this water be grace for your thirsting soul as it fills your entire being . . . sit for a moment and enjoy the wonder of the water within your well. . . .

Now slowly return to this time and place.

Integrative Process

Take time to draw your well. Don't worry about whether you are an artist or not. This is not about having something "look good." It's about recognizing and naming some of the truth and goodness that is found in your inner well.

Once you have created your well, draw a symbol or write a phrase in your well for each of the following:

- something that nourishes and energizes you
- something that needs to be released and healed
- something that desires to be shared with the cosmos
- something that longs to be celebrated

After your well has been created and you have named what you've found in your well, find someone to share what you have discovered.

Ritual

The following body movements can be done to conclude this well meditation after sharing has taken place. It is a good way to acknowledge and celebrate what has been drawn up from the inner well.

Nourish: Imagine you are dipping into the well with your hands shaped as a cup. Hold the cup to your mouth with the action of drinking and savoring.

Heal: Dip in again. Imagine this time that you bring the water up and let it wash over you—over your head, shoulders, heart, breasts, torso . . . especially any place that cries out for healing.

Unite: Imagine you have a chalice in your hands. Fill the chalice with water from your well, turn slowly in a full circle, hold out the water to all who yearn for peace.

Celebrate: Imagine that you dip in again. Bring the water up with your chalice. Dance freely with the water. Sprinkle those around you with water from the well. End with a deep bow.

Fall Cleaning

A Guided Meditation

Give each participant an autumn leaf that has fallen from a tree.

Introduction

We often hear people talk about spring cleaning. Spring seems to be a traditional time to do a thorough house cleaning or to take a look inside closets and discern how we need to rid our lives of clutter. The season of autumn is also a good time to unclutter. Nature is busy doing her own house cleaning in this season of transformation and relinquishment.

Meditation

Look at the leaf in your hand. Once it belonged to a tree. It hung from a branch. The tree and the branch that were once home for this leaf are now barren. Somewhere that barren tree stands, but the leaf has come to rest in your hand.

Now imagine the leaf still hanging on the tree to which it once belonged. With the eye of your heart see it blowing in the breeze still green; keep your eyes on the leaf while it gradually changes from green to red and gold. Perhaps it even turns brown and crumbly before it lets go. Finally it detaches itself from its tree home. Watch it as it slowly makes its journey to the ground. Is it still speaking in bright colors, or has it already changed to an earthen brown? What caused it to let go? Was it the rain, or a storm or maybe a gentle wind?

Or, was it just the right time for it to fall? Whatever your leaf's history might be, it has now come to rest in your hand.

Let the leaf now speak to you about your own need to let go.

- Look into your closets. What do you see? Are there things you haven't worn or used for years? In what way do you need to simplify? *(Pause.)*

- Look around your house, your room. What meets your eye? Do you see things that are only taking up space? Things you are not enjoying? Not using? Books you aren't reading? Do you know someone else who might enjoy them? Sometimes the material things you let go of are symbolic of inner work you need to do. *(Pause.)*

- Let's look now at your inner closets. What do you see? Would you experience a greater freedom if you were able to surrender certain attitudes, harmful ways of thinking, anxieties? What needs to fall from the tree of your life? *(Pause.)*

- What do you need to relinquish? Resentments, bitterness, hostility? *(Pause.)*

- What is it that crowds out your joy, smothers your love, or takes away your peace? Indifference, apathy, boredom? *(Pause.)*

- Is there anything crowding out your delight? Your enthusiasm? Fear, anxiety, busyness? *(Pause.)*

At this time of house cleaning you may have noticed some things that you would like to see cleaned out of your inner or outer closets. Gently hold those things in your hand. Ask the leaf in your hand to cradle them and to help you know what to surrender.

What needs your attention? What kind of action do you need to take? What would facilitate the fall house cleaning you desire? Do you need to take a risk? Share with someone? Ask for support? Go for counseling? *(Pause.)*

Closing

Now take your leaf and hold it up slightly as an offering during our closing prayer.

O Breath of God, this leaf is my life! Come with your transforming breath. Descend from the heavens; rise up out of the earth. Surround me with your liberating breath. Free me from the things that keep me tied only to what I know. Reveal to me the things that hinder, those things that prevent me from being a blessing in the lives of others. Take away my leaves of resentment, fear, apathy, indifference, greed. Help me to surrender my self-hatred and discouragement. Empty me that there may be a beautiful new space in me for renewal. I offer you this leaf of my life. Receive me.

Entering the Heart of Autumn

Begin by relaxing. Let your spirit rest . . . gently let go of busy things in your mind . . . allow your body to slow down. . . . Take a deep breath and let it out slowly. Do this three times. Gradually sink into a quiet place of ease and comfort.

Move into your inner self . . . when you are inside, visualize a peaceful and inviting wooded area. . . . There is a trail that meanders through the trees. Look for it. When you find it, begin to walk on this narrow path. . . . As you walk along, notice that it is autumn. The air feels cooler. . . . Hear the crunch of the dry leaves beneath your feet. . . . Smell the odor of tree bark and dry leaves. . . . See the sunlight coming through the trees. . . . Everywhere you glance, see magnificent colored leaves of gold, rust, orange, and yellow. . . . Look up and see little gusts of wind twirl more leaves to the ground. . . .

You now come to a widening of the path that leads to a circle of oak trees. . . . In this circle there is an old wooden bench. Go to the bench and sit down. Abide there and let the mellow beauty of the woods penetrate your whole being. . . .

As you sit in the woods, reflect on your life. Ponder the part of your life that feels satisfying and rewarding: the dimension of it that is like the plenitude and fullness of an autumn harvest, the part that is mellow and fulfilling. . . .

Now you look at the leaves hanging on the branches. Watch a leaf as it breaks free from a twig and twirls to the ground. . . . As you watch, become aware of a part of your life that is also hanging on a branch, about to break free and fall to the ground. See what it is that you need to let go of, what can no longer be a part of your life. Take time to be with this. . . .

What does it feel like to be there among the beauty of the trees with their dying leaves falling to the ground? Is it consoling? . . . Does it hurt? . . . Is it helpful? . . . Is it challenging? . . . Does it encourage you? . . .

Finally, you arise from the bench in the woods to go back the way you came. But before you leave the circle of trees, stoop down and pick up one leaf. . . . Notice what color and shape it is. Hold it to your cheek and feel the texture of it. . . . Lay it carefully in the palm of one of your hands. Now begin the journey on the path toward home. . . .

As you arrive at the entrance to the woods, turn around and look once more at the autumn trees. . . . Look at the leaf in your hand. Let it fall to the ground. Leave it behind to celebrate your desire and willingness to let go and grow. . . . Now hear a message that stirs your heart. What is this message? . . . Repeat it slowly and quietly to yourself.

Gently come back to this time and place. Take time to write down anything you would like to remember from your time in the woods.

Questions for individual reflection

1. What is most satisfying and fulfilling for you at this time of your life?

2. How have you experienced the dying of autumn in your personal growth?

3. What do you fear to let go of?

4. What kind of help or support do you need in order to do the letting go that is being asked of you?

5. How does the message you heard as you left the woods relate to what is currently happening in your life?

Integration

Go for a walk and gather some autumn leaves (or draw, or paint them).

Let each leaf represent some part of your life's journey where you had to let go of someone or something in order to grow (a child leaving home, a change of attitude, loss of a job, an illness, a death . . .).

Give a name to each of these leaves, one for each of your significant autumn experiences. Drop each leaf into a basket, calling out its name as you do so. Keep the basket with you for the season of autumn. Look at it often, remembering how each of these autumns required you to lose something in order to gain something new for your growth.

The Deep Well of Your Life

A Celebration of Our Individual and Communal Wells of Wisdom

As a central focus, create a "well" into which participants can pour water. Place a pitcher or clay jar in a large bowl. As the water is poured into the pitcher, it eventually flows over into the bowl.

Give everyone an empty plastic glass.

Introduction

Look into the empty space of this glass. With your hand, touch the emptiness inside. There is hidden potential in emptiness. The vacant space suggests that there is room for something new. See yourself as a vessel full of open space for what is yet to come. When you are willing to hand over the open space of your life you will discover a deep well of inner wisdom.

The Gift of Water

Ask all to raise their glass, a gesture of handing over their lives as vessels to be filled and poured out. Use a chant that can easily be taught to the group. A suggestion is "Into Your Hands I Commit" from the CD Holy Ground by Monica Brown. After the chant, leaders fill the glasses with water.

In this glass there is a community of molecules. Each drop of water has a history. If only it could tell the story of where it has been. Perhaps:

- a sparkling diamond of dew on a blade of grass,

- hanging over some country pond in the form of mist,

- sleeping in the depths of the ocean,

- part of a laughing waterfall,

- living in a flowing river,

- rushing over rocks in a mountain stream,

- falling rain on a thirsty garden,

- dripping from forest branches.

We can only imagine its history. It has now found a home in the glass you are holding.

  A brief silence

In memory of this sacred water's history, please echo after me these words from David Whyte's poem: "Where Many Waters Meet."

All the water below me came from above
All the clouds living in the mountains
gave it to the rivers
who gave it to the sea
which was their dying.

And so I float on cloud become water
central sea surrounded by white mountains,
the water salt, once fresh,
cloud fall and stream rush,
tree roots and tide bank
leading to the rivers' mouths

and the mouths of the river sing into the sea,

the stories buried in the mountains

give out into the sea

and the sea remembers

and sings back from the depths

where nothing is forgotten.

A brief silence

A Prayer to the Sacred Waters

Think of yourself as a chalice.

We turn to the west holding out the chalice of our life

that we may be filled with the life-giving waters of wisdom,

that we may be cleansed and refreshed so that, in return,

we, too, may bless and refresh others.

O all you sacred bodies of water throughout the earth,

you whom we cannot live without,

flow, waters, flow!

Flow into the chalice of each life represented here.

Flow, waters, flow:

oceans and lakes, rivers and fountains,

mountain streams, running brooks,

quiet pools in the forests, underground springs,

deep wells and reservoirs, raindrops and tears.

Flow, waters, flow! Flow over us

renewing our spirits, transforming our lives,

calming our emotions, balancing our lives,

flow into the chalice of our bodies.

Mingle with the water that makes up our body.

You holy, sacred water, flowing miracle of grace,

we honor you.

A brief silence

Reading

We focus now on our individual call to be wells of wisdom. Out of the reservoir of our lives, living water flows out to a thirsty world. Each of us has the potential to be a well of refreshment for others. Listen carefully to the words of the following poem entitled "On Being a Well."

What makes this world so lovely

is that somewhere it hides a well.

Something lovely there is about a well

so deep

unpiped and real

filled

with buckets and buckets

of that life-giving drink.

A faucet will do in a hurry,

but what makes the world so lovely

is that somewhere

it hides a well!

Sometimes
people are like wells
deep and real
natural (unpiped)
life-giving
calm and cool
refreshing.

They bring out what is best in you
They are like fountains of pure joy
They make you want to sing, or maybe dance.
They encourage you to laugh
even, when things get rough.
And maybe that's why
things never stay rough
once you've found a well.

Some experiences are like wells too.
People create them
They are life-giving happenings
They are redeeming experiences
They are wells,
wells of wonder
wells of hope.
When you find a well
and you will some day,
Drink deeply of the gift within.
And then maybe soon
you'll discover

that you've become
what you've received,
and then you'll be a well
for others to find.

So lift up your eyes
and look all around you:
> Over the mountains, down in the valley
> out in the ocean, over the runways
> into the cities, into the country
> sidewalks and highways
> paths in the forest
> into the hearts of a thirsty people.

Look!
And I beg you
don't ever stop looking
because what makes this world so lovely
is that somewhere
it hides a well,
a well that hasn't been found yet.

And if you don't find it
maybe
nobody will!

And if you don't be one
maybe
nobody will find you!

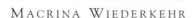

MACRINA WIEDERKEHR

Water Ritual

Celebrating Our Individual Well of Wisdom

Invite participants now to drink symbolically from the well of their lives as you slowly lead them through the following reflection:

Raise the glass to your mouth. Feel the water moisten your lips. Drink deeply and gratefully from the well of your life. Experience this life-giving gift of water going down your throat and entering your stomach. About two-thirds of your body is water. About seventy percent of your skin is water; eighty-three percent of your blood is water. Water is the one natural resource that we, along with the plants and animals, need for living. You, too, have gifts from your inner well that the world needs for survival. Recall your first home in the watery womb of your mother. Let your memory go further back to the sea water from which your ancestors emerged. Be one with the water.

Celebrating Our Communal Well of Wisdom

You have drunk from the richness of your inner well. Now you are called to remember that the gift you have received you must give. Thus you are invited to come to the well and pour the water from your individual well into our communal well.

In the monastic tradition there is a lovely practice of preparation for Vespers called "*statio.*" This Latin word means *standing* together. Before processing into chapel, the monks stand together for a few moments of remembering the sacredness of the moment, who they are and what they are about to do. After a short period of standing in silence, a procession into chapel begins. They bow to the sanctuary,

216

then turn to their partners and bow to the Christ in that person. It is this spirit we would like to create here.

Please stand! We stand in silence acknowledging the holiness of this moment. We remember our own inner resources, our gifts for sharing, our own deep well of wisdom.

After a few moments of standing in silence, all are invited to come to the well. Ask participants to come with a partner. They are to pour their glass of water into the inner pitcher, listening to the sound of the splashing water. Then turning to one another, they behold the Christ in the other and honor that person with a profound bow. If the group is large, participants can be invited to come in small groups rather than with a single partner.

All form a circle around the well.

We have owned our individual wells of wisdom. We have honored the ageless well of our communal wisdom. In honor of all the "living wells" here present, let us sing a song of gratitude, a song that binds us together as one.

Song

"Flow, River, Flow," (*Each Time I Think of You*, Bob Hurd).

Carrying Autumn in My Heart

This book provides a ritual for each season of the year based on the ancient custom of honoring the four directions of Earth. They use similar symbols to represent the directions, but the text of the prayers for each season is different. The prayers are focused on each particular season. The following ritual celebrates autumn. You will need these symbols: feather, candle, pitcher of water, bowl of soil, dry weeds, dead flowers, seeds. Each of the prayers below can be prayed by various leaders or by the entire group.

East

Hold a feather up in the air and let it fall to the ground as a sign of surrender and letting go.

Great Spirit of the East,
I stand before the place of rising sun,
knowing the time to let go has arrived.
The chill of this seasonal change
challenges my hopeful dreams.
A persistent voice in me nudges
my tough hold on inner security.
Bless me with the rays of your love
as I struggle with my desires and needs.
May autumn's brilliant colors
give me hope for the days ahead.

South

Light a candle. Let it burn for a minute. Then blow it out as a sign of the darkness approaching.

Great Spirit of the South,

I turn to you with nostalgic awareness.

Summer's flowers are gasping goodbye.

Baskets of abundance sigh with farewell.

Now comes the season of diminishment.

The rays of the sun are more distant

and the vibrant greens are turning gray.

Now arrives the time of surrender.

May your love settle quietly in me

like a mother bear entering the cave.

West

Hold a pitcher that has just an inch or so of water in it. Pour even this little bit of water out onto the ground or into an old bowl or a container that needs to be discarded.

Great Spirit of the West,

I bow to the place of goodbye,

where the sun slides below the horizon.

I stand in the presence of the ancestors

whose wisdom invites me further.

As they learned from their transitions,

so will I look to the teachings of this time.

I will fall into the embrace of emptiness,

trusting new life to emerge.

Draw me near as my fullness slips away.

North

Place dry weeds, or dead flowers with seeds, on top of the bowl filled with soil.

Great Spirit of the North,
the land is stripped of what was strong.
The long months of waiting soon begin.
I move toward a vigil of emptiness.
Keep alive the memory of harvested seeds
while autumn stretches frosty fingers
around the corners of my watchful heart.
I will enter the lengthy darkness
with the strong arms of your love
wrapped around my waiting heart.

A Celebration of the Autumn Equinox

Gather around a large table layered with colorful autumn cloths of gold, tan, orange, rust, wine, on which are placed several large baskets, or a cornucopia, filled to overflowing with local fruits, vegetables, grains, wines, jams, etc. A large candle burns on each of the four corners. Soft lamplight filters through the room as a reminder of the dimming of light at this time of year.

Introduction

Many indigenous people associate autumn with the direction of the west because it is the place of the setting sun. The autumnal equinox occurs on the day when the sun crosses the equator, as it did for the spring equinox, creating approximately equal light and darkness on this day. In spring, this movement signaled a future increase in the sun's light. Now it signals a lessening of sunlight's energy, a movement toward slowing down.

Like the setting sun slipping beyond the horizon, so the autumned earth slips slowly toward a night-like season of extended darkness. From now on there will be less light and more darkness until the winter solstice when the sunlight will once more begin to increase with each day. But for now the autumnal equinox beckons us into the twilight, into longer nights and shorter days.

The autumnal equinox is also a time to honor the abundance and bounty of the earth as we move toward the less productive, leaner months of winter. Now is a good moment to gather our thanks. Now is the time to remember that we have what we need to give us strength and nourishment during barren, fallow times.

Let us lean toward the twilight, opening our spirits to the soft, resonant space of eveningtide.

Song

"Let Evening Fall" (*Gift of God*, Marty Haughen) or "You Are There" (*We Are the Circle*, Julie Howard) or any other song related to evening time/setting sun.

Hearing the Call to Let Go

The leader now reads this brief guided visualization:

Find a comfortable posture and let yourself sink into the moment. Close your eyes. Breathe easily and freely. . . . Let yourself sigh . . . loosen your grip on any thoughts that want to keep you occupied. . . .

Go inside now and imagine you are sitting someplace where it is dusk. You are watching the sun set. See the huge red ball of fire as it slips slowly downward. Notice the color of the clouds on the horizon. . . . Continue gazing until you can no longer see the sun. . . . Now it is twilight. Linger there, feeling safe and content. . . . Hear the birds calling to one another one last time before they fly to their nests for the night. . . . It is an easy, gentle moment for you. Continue sitting there while gradually you see less and less around you. . . . Feel the air becoming cooler. . . . Night will soon come. . . .

As you sit there, you become aware of something in your life that is sinking beyond the horizon, something that needs to be let go. . . . Watch this part of your life as it moves, like the sun, beyond your sight. . . . Let it go from you as light goes at the end of the day. . . . Let it go from you as summer goes and autumn comes. . . . Encourage your heart to let go of whatever it needs to. . . .

Receive the comforting presence of evening, the mellow air and the gentle presence of earth settling in for the night. . . . Let the spirit of autumn speak to your heart . . . receive whatever you need to enter into your own autumn. . . . Now, gradually return to this time and place.

Autumn Pronouncement

All stand

Earth is shedding the abundance of summer. Leaves fall from the trees. Sunlight lessens. Everywhere there is a move toward letting go. Join with me as we enter into the spirit of autumn.

Repeat after the leader:

I am the sun setting in the west.

I am the tree letting go of the leaves.

I am the harvest taken from the land.

I am the bird winging swiftly southward.

Spirit Keeper of the West,

I will enter into the heart of autumn.

I will bravely enter my transitions.

I will adapt to what needs changing.

I will freely let go and not hang on.

Come, Spirit of Autumn, and teach me!

Gathering Our Abundance

Each one comes forth and receives an item from the baskets or the cornucopia. Ask them to look at this item of harvest, to think of the journey it has taken since it was springtime. Following this, ask them to take a time of quiet to ponder these questions:

Is there a part of your life that holds abundance?

If so, what is this abundance? How has it blessed you?

Is there a part of your life that has matured and come to greater fullness?

How did this maturation process happen?

Dialogue

Gather in small groups to talk about each one's abundance. Following this sharing time, form one large circle and stand. The leader invites each one to call out an abundance that has come to them during the year. This could be followed by sitting and listening to or singing the chant: "I Am Thankful," (Many Voiced Angel, Velma Frye).

Turn off the lights now and have only the candles on the table burning as a signal of autumn's increasing darkness. Sit in a circle. Join hands. Listen to "Deep Peace" as a way of entering into autumn (Songs for the Inner Child, Shaina Noll).

Closing

Close with a quiet blessing after the group mingles and whispers to one another:

May autumn lead you into deeper peace.

Winter

Season

of

Waiting

Introduction to Winter

Winter is a lesson about the fine art of loss and growth.

Its lesson is clear; There is only one way out of struggle

and that is by going into its darkness,

waiting for the light, and being open to new growth.

JOAN CHITTISTER

In winter, the heartbeat of the land slows to alpha pace. The eyes of this season are drowsy. Sleepy limbs of nature fold in upon themselves to rest during long months of inactivity. This is the period of dormancy when the extravagance of summer becomes a distant memory. In places where the land and water are frozen, the cold solidity adds to the non-movement and stillness. Life waits, subdued and hidden in mystery, humbled by the pervasive strength of winter's presence.

As the days of light get shorter and shorter, there is an invitation to an unhurried pace in the circle of life. The barren branches are hushed. Hibernating creatures snuggle in their protective homes, and seeds of all sorts bow their heads to the soil's quietness. Nature accepts the great change that the pilgrimage of Earth brings. Now is not the time for stretching and growing. Now is the time for withdrawal and restoration of energy.

The lessening of light and the increase of darkness are necessary ingredients for the earth's nourishment. They enable the fallow process to happen. Nature has been busy producing. It is time to slow down and rest. Without this rest, soil wears out and loses its nutrients. All of creation needs some time to pause and have its spent energy renewed. So do humans. Winter offers this gift of essential renewal.

Like every other season, winter holds a beauty all its own. In spite of the fact that numerous warm-blooded folks do not take kindly to this season, there is much to wonder and be amazed at in the world of winter. It is less busy and more reflective, offering space to snuggle close to loved ones, read a good book, engage in a favorite indoor activity, or relax by a fireplace in the long evenings of darkness.

Winter brings a certain solace in the great hush that settles over a thriving city after a heavy snowfall. When it encases everything in a sparkling glaze of transparency after an ice-storm, this season displays an astounding beauty. Winter's best side shows in midnight-blue skies, crisp invigorating air, brilliant stars, snow-lined tree limbs, fluffy feathered birds, footprints of deer hooves and rabbit paws, frosted designs on window panes, and the invigorating winter sports of skiing and snowboarding, ice skating, hockey, and snowmobiling. There is also the traditional rolling of snowballs to create snowpersons on the front lawn, or lying down in the velvety softness to make snow angels.

Winter has its share of beauty, but it also has its share of harshness. Even though it is quiet and dormant, it sometimes manifests a pronounced and damaging intensity which is of special concern to the vulnerable and the homeless. Winter moves along in an easy, almost inconspicuous manner until, like a grouchy grizzly bear awakened too early from sleep, it rises up with fury, pouncing on the land with force. Bone chilling temperatures, terror-inducing blizzards, loss of electricity, broken tree limbs laden with ice, heavy flooding, and life-threatening car accidents are part of this destructive side of winter.

Because of the uncomfortable conditions of winter, it is natural to underestimate the positive value of this season. The same is true for our interior winters. Few consider their inner wintertime something to enjoy, yet this season is vital for spiritual growth. The human spirit needs dormancy and rest, silence and solitude. Winter provides this opportunity so we can slow down and refocus our direction and purpose in life.

We also encounter storms and prolonged hard times during our interior winters. This season challenges us out of our comfort zones. Courage to stand strong, faith to maintain a positive outlook, and hope for the future are all stored in the rhythms of winter. The extended darkness of our inner winter can be an opportunity to learn more about ourselves and our relationship with God. The fury of winter storms forces us to let go of our securities. It causes us to reach out for help from others when our strength is frail and our spirit lacks the confidence to go on.

In the interior wintertime we can easily lose heart, stop believing in our goodness, forget about our resilience, and discount the presence of those who love us. There is often sadness, loneliness, and a depletion of joy. This is the season of grief and depression, of searching and struggle. Dreams and vision of what could be are hidden from us. Enthusiasm wanes. Our passion for life is stripped from us like a barren winter branch. This Gethsemane-like period taunts the wintered heart with a persistent fear that we will never again feel good about ourselves or about life.

Sometimes our interior winter is not fraught with sorrow or utter desolation. It is, instead, filled with emptiness, an extended fallow time when it seems as though nothing at all is happening. Life is dull. Everything seems to be at a standstill. We doubt our growth. Our inner landscape appears bleak and empty.

Winter is the season of waiting. It requires great trust and a willingness to believe that this angst will not last forever. Even though all appears dead and void of movement, there is quiet growth taking place. During the darkness, gestation occurs. In the caves and hidden hollows of winter, baby bears are born. In the frozen air, branches with terminal buds secretly grow every day. In the unmoving soil, flower bulbs are strengthened for their future journey upward toward the sun. In the frozen human heart, the silent seeds of confidence are prepared for amazing new growth.

While we are in our winter space, we may be tempted to give up, to lose hope, to stop believing in ourselves and in the presence of the Holy One because we cannot see our growth. Winter asks us only to be, to live with mystery, to wait patiently. We are required to keep a delicate balance between yielding to winter's silence and keeping our eyes on a future springtime. Each day challenges us to carry hope in our hearts no matter how sparse our awareness of inner stirrings might be.

This gruff-voiced season has another voice less readily heard. It is the calm and wise voice of encouragement. Winter offers assurance that the seeds of life are being tended, that what is needed for future growth is simply waiting to burst forth with the wild joy of spring. And spring will, indeed, come. For just as every other season eventually departs, so, too, will winter. It will return again when it is time, for each season's entrance and departure is part of the turning in the great circle of life.

Winter Darkness

······································

Winter darkness
swaddles the long evenings
with comforting covers of stillness,
greets the brightness of the waxing moon,
fills the clear royal blue sky
with brilliant patterns of shining stars,
applauds the vigor of determined dawns,
receives the bowed head of setting sun.

Winter darkness

nestles close in the heart of wine cellars,
envelops dreams of dozing bears,
soothes the fallow frozen land,
grants flower bulbs needed time
to catch their husky breath,
lingers gratefully in resting soil
and lullabies the hidden seeds.

Winter darkness

allows owls longer hours to hunt,
gives creatures room to roam freely,
lets the moon dance her fullness
in the shadowed elbows of leafless trees,
sings the silence of peacefulness,

joins hands with the dancing light
of the amazing aurora borealis.

Something in my human psyche
keeps wanting to light up the darkness,
to stay away from the silent shadows
and steer clear from thick, black nights.

Perhaps I have not spent enough time
holding hands with long winter evenings.
Not all darkness demands a shining candle
held before its coal black eyes.

——————

JOYCE RUPP

A Winter Blessing

Blessed are you, winter,
dark season of waiting,
you affirm the dark seasons of our lives,
forecasting the weather of waiting in hope.

Blessed are you, winter,
you faithfully guard a life unseen,
calling those who listen deeply
to discover winter rest.

Blessed are you, winter,
frozen and cold on the outside,
within your silent, nurturing womb
you warmly welcome all that longs for renewal.

Blessed are you, winter,
your bleak, barren trees
preach wordless sermons
about emptiness and solitude.

Blessed are you, winter,
you teach us valuable lessons
about waiting in darkness
with hope and trust.

Blessed are you, winter,
season of blood red sunsets

and star-filled, long, dark nights,
faithfully you pour out your beauty.

Blessed are you, winter,
when your tiny snowflakes
flurry through the air,
you awaken our sleeping souls.

Blessed are you, winter,
with your wild and varied moods,
so intent on being yourself,
you refuse to be a people-pleaser.

Blessed are you, winter,
when ice storms crush our hearts and homes,
you call forth the good in us
as we rush to help one another.

Blessed are you, winter,
your inconsistent moods
often challenge spring's arrival,
yet how gracefully you step aside
when her time has come.

Holy Darkness Prayer

Darkness is a beautiful gift although it is often equated with sin and evil. The seed in the earth must have darkness in order to grow. We were fashioned and formed in the darkness of our mother's womb. After a day of hard work it is good to turn off the light and let the darkness bring sleep to our eyes. Only when it is dark can we see the wondrous night sky with its display of moon, stars and planets. Lovers welcome the darkness as a time to be with the beloved. In this prayer, we honor the fruitful darkness of our lives, the comforting and restful darkness, the nurturing darkness.

After each prayer, participants echo the leader's
"We praise you, O Holy Darkness."

Dear Fruitful Ground of our Being, you turn the sun's face away from us as you gather us into the darkness of winter. You call us inside to the great fires in our hearts, those fires we have never believed in. You ask us to warm the hands of hope in our secret soul places. You show us the heaven seeds that have been planted in our souls, and you remind us that heaven's answers rest in the dark ground of our beings.

Response: We praise you, O Holy Darkness.

Dear Fruitful Ground of our Being, when the deep loneliness comes, you cradle us in your enriching dark arms. In the darkness you teach us to trust in what we cannot see, to hope for that which seems impossible, to have faith in the night of unknowing. You reveal to us the necessity of patience and the holiness of waiting in the dark as we enter into solitude.

Response: We praise you, O Holy Darkness.

Dear Fruitful Ground of our Being, in the darkness you cover us with beauty: the poetry of the moon and stars, the loveliness of nocturnal creatures who make music in the forest's darkness, the mystery of silvery shadows. You soften the day's light to show us the light of night. You give us the gift of rest and sleep. You send us your night angel to close our tired eyes and breathe dreams and visions into our longing hearts.

Response: We praise you, O Holy Darkness.

Dear Fruitful Ground of our Being, once upon a time in the holy darkness of our mother's womb, we waited for birth. Now we are being born again. We are growing wings in our sorrow's darkness and finding new eyes that can see in the dark. On your black, earthy pillow we rest our heads and hearts. We trust your unseen blessings.

Response: We praise you, O Holy Darkness.

Dear Fruitful Ground of our Being, all of creation finds life in the watery womb of your darkness. Deep in the rich black soil of the earth many happy seeds are cradled in your nurturing womb. Soon the shell of the seed will crack open and blessings will rise up out of the darkness.

Response: We praise you, O Holy Darkness.
Let us pray (pause).

O God, in the quiet darkness of this moment we search for the sacred light that shines on in our darkness. Just as we find this light in you, O God, help us understand that deep in the recesses of our souls, light shines. Thank you for all the things that grow in darkness. To find the light we must go into the dark. Go with us into all the dark places where we must travel. Take away our fear of darkness. Be a lantern for us that we may be lanterns for one another.

Childhood Memories of Winter

The winters of my childhood that I remember most vividly are the years before we had indoor plumbing and television. I do not recall feeling deprived during those years. Winter was simply a part of life, one of the four seasons, and it seemed natural to adapt to the way that winter expressed itself.

We had lots of snow, mounds of it, in fact. I had to wear high boots to walk around the farmyard. Dad would plow us out after every snowstorm. He had a loader on the front end of the tractor, and he'd dump the snow in huge mountain-like piles. These mounds were great fun to play on, and they occupied a lot of time for my siblings and me. I can still feel the cold of those winters: my chapped hands and cheeks after playing in the snow, making snow angels, digging all morning to create a tunnel, and playing fox and goose.

I liked to walk in the grove and see the tracks of rabbits, squirrels, raccoons, and other animals. I'd follow their patterns along for a while until the snow was too deep for me or the tracks ran under a fence or too far out into the fields.

The smells of winter are more memorable than the feeling of coldness. The freshness of winter air was invigorating, clean, and clear. I loved coming into the farmhouse with the delicious odor of my mother's homemade soup wafting through the opened door. There were also days, usually Saturday mornings, when Mom would bake bread. She would take some of the raised dough, fry it in lard, and dip it in sugar. It was a treat from heaven. We would eat as much as we could after we had taken some out to Dad, who was always working on repairing something in the machine shop.

Then, there was the odor of the cattle in the barn. When I reached the age of ten, it was my job to feed them hay each day. This meant climbing a tall ladder to the loft and tossing down bales of hay into the manger below. When I opened the barn door the stench of urine filled my nostrils. If it was a really cold day, I could see the clouds of moisture from the steers' breath. They might be huddled close together for warmth, but once I got inside they knew it was time for a meal and quickly lined up at the manger. When I was up in the loft, the smell of the sweet, aged alfalfa in the bales of hay took over my senses. I never minded that job. It was a warm place and there was a kind of quiet joy in it, knowing I was feeding those hungry animals.

In mid-winter, it was always dark by the time we finished the chores outside. Many times I would leave the barn just in time to see the sun setting in the west through the grove of cottonwood and walnut trees. The winter sky was often a cool blue-gray with shining peach and purple threads across it. I have always loved this time of day and I would pause, even then, to gaze at the beauty of the western sky.

In the deepest part of winter, the sun had already set and the stars would be strong in the clear blue sky. The stars easily spoke to me, something wordless I could never have named, but powerful and comforting at the same time. It was like old friends greeting and blessing me as I walked from the barn to the house.

Some things I did not enjoy about winter, like trudging to the outhouse and freezing inside on that cold seat. Or getting dressed in the morning. I shared a bedroom with my sisters and the only heat we had in our room in the wintertime was what came up through a grate in the floor. We'd stand over that grate, shivering and shaking while we quickly dressed. I couldn't wait to get downstairs and stand by the coal stove once I'd gotten out of bed.

What I experienced and learned about winter in my youth is that it was natural, normal, to have the dark, the cold, the snow. I went with the flow of the season, took it in stride, and rarely complained or whined about it. Winter was just winter and it brought its own unique colors, feelings, and challenges. I have especially longed for those childhood days of acceptance when I've found my adult-self fighting the natural unfolding of the season.

Winter also brought me my most satisfying times with my father. It was on those long wintry nights that Dad would sit in his easy chair reading. If we were lucky, one of us children would get to come and sit next to Dad as he read. We knew that we had to be quiet as a mouse and not disturb him. Every once in a while he'd pause and tease me with a pat, a whisker rub, or a fake nudge of trying to boost me out of "the nest." I loved the feeling of being squeezed in there close to my Dad, feeling his presence even though it was a silent one.

Perhaps that is why I now lean into winter with a certain relish. It never used to be that way, but as I have grown older, I have returned to quiet moments like those of being in the winter chair by my father's side. I see the value of "being" and the purpose of silence. I realize that presence in itself is a treasure. I have learned to welcome the evenings of darkness as a cozy time for my own silent space of renewal and relaxation.

JOYCE RUPP

All Through the Night

All through the night
into the morning hours
cold beads of rain
ice the tree's dark branches.

The trees are strong; they do not bend
and this becomes their downfall.
When you do not bend, you break.
The icy day becomes my classroom.

Near the ice sculptured trees
frozen little bushes, vines, and cedars
are bowed low in adoration,
bent, but not broken.

The frozen trees, sad and beautiful,
moan and sway with the weight of reality.
Lovely ice sculptured arms
yield to the bitter truth of the moment
as the silence is harshly broken.

In its wake, a deafening silence
rises up from deep inside
where my tears are frozen
like the beads of rain
that fell through the night.

How do we name what happens
without condemning it?
This is nature's way;
there were no developers present.

Was the rain unkind to freeze?
Did it have a choice?
Do we have a choice
to bend or break,
to destroy or build?

Sometimes I fear reality.

MACRINA WIEDERKEHR

The Wintered Spirit

How can you believe in the softness of a flower petal when your heart has turned to stone?

How can you dream of an easy rain when all your love is frozen in glaciers of loss?

How can you hope for fruit to form on the tree when you can hardly hang on to life each day?

How can you find the promise in a seed when your heart is lost in the depths of depression?

How can you sense the stirrings of a butterfly when your energy is cocooned in sorrow?

It takes immense trust and hope to see new life waiting beneath the frozen, barren land.

It takes deep courage to remain in the cave of loneliness and painful solitude.

It takes powerful faith to believe in the gestation of a positive future when all is unknown.

It takes compassionate patience to remain by the side of an aching seed in the silent soil.

It takes stout-hearted resilience to endure the soul's contractions of seemingly endless birthing.

It takes vulnerable openness to stay present to deadness and not run from staleness.

We wait for new life, but we do not wait alone.

We wait with the mother bear as the little cub within her takes shape and form.

We wait with the dormant juices of the maple trees gathering up sweetness in their empty limbs.

We wait with the grapes in the vat fermenting and turning themselves into full, red wine.

We wait with the pruned rose bushes sighing for warming sun to sing them into budding.

We wait with the frozen creeks and rivers yearning to be melted into laughing waters.

We wait with all humans whose weary lives turn slowly toward re-awakened joy.

We wait with the cosmos which is ever dying and being reborn, giving away and receiving anew.

And while we wait, we struggle to accept winter as a necessary companion, an inner season calling us to be more than we now are, a confident guide taking us on a perilous journey that is part of every dying and every birthing.

It is in the winter of our lives that the enduring Voice within coaxes us along, nudges us into belief, urges us to stay in the dark for as long as it takes for re-birthing to occur.

In our wintered time, it is this One who draws us close, nestles us near to heart, breathes strength into our spiritual bones, and assures us that we are growing wings under the frozen land of our desolate and emptied self.

JOYCE RUPP

The Singing Darkness

Far from the city's lights
the darkness is free to be dark.
Even the stars creep respectfully
into their caves of clouds
as if to honor the dark.
The trees hold their breath.
Not even a leaf falls,
nothing breaks the silence.

A nurturing, comforting darkness
surrounds me; I lean into it,
terrified with joy,
remembering my birth
from the womb of darkness.

Out of the darkness
a song once arose, akin
to the song of the first creation.
In that dark singing womb I ripened,
blessed and cradled by the darkness.

The Singing Darkness
filled me with melodies
until I became a song.
The Singing Darkness
carried me into the dawn and
sent me forth to sing my own song.

Tonight I honor the darkness
and sing of the life I was given
in the holy darkness of my first home,
that nurturing, earthy womb
where I grew bright with life
and blossomed in God.

MACRINA WIEDERKEHR

Listening to Winter

The trees have shed their colorful autumn robes.
Winter is raging through the dark, empty branches
and I am listening.
I am listening to the roar and to the quiet of winter.
I am listening to a beauty
that sometimes remains unseen.

*I am listening.**

I am listening to the seed hidden in the earth.
I am listening to the dark swallowing up the light.
I am listening to faith rising out of doubt.
I am listening to the need to believe without seeing.

I am listening.

I am listening to the season of contemplation,
to the urgency of our world's need for reflection.
I am listening to all that waits within the earth,
to bulbs and seeds,
to deep roots dreaming.
I am listening to the sacred, winter rest.

I am listening.

I am listening to long nights,
comforting darkness,
fruitful darkness,

beautiful darkness.

I am listening to the darkness of the winter season.

I am listening to the sparks of hope within the darkness.

I am listening.

I am listening to storms raging out my window,

to storms raging in my heart.

I am listening to all that makes me pull my cloak a little tighter.

I am listening to trust buried deep in the ground of my being.

I am listening.

I am listening to the kind permission of the season

to rest more often,

to reflect more deeply,

to pray without words.

I am listening to the sacrament of non-doing.

I am listening.

I am listening to my dreams and inner visions,

to the unknown wrapped in the mystery of my life,

to tears trapped in underground streams of my being,

to seeds watered daily by those tears.

I am listening.

I am listening to the quiet life in winter's womb.

I am listening to winter, nurturing spring.

I am listening to brilliant winter sunsets

and lovely frosty mornings.

I am listening to snowflakes flying through the air,

to the cold winds that often blow out there,

to bare trees, so lovely in their emptiness,

to one leaf that never did let go.

I am listening.

I am listening to winter

handing over spring.

I am listening to the poetry of winter.

I am listening.

MACRINA WIEDERKEHR

*If this poem is used for a group service, an option is to have participants echo after the leader the italicized *I am listening* that follows each stanza.

Winter's Cloak

This year I do not want
the dark to leave me.
I need its wrap
of silent stillness,
its cloak
of long lasting embrace.
Too much light
has pulled me away
from the chamber
of gestation.

Let the dawns
come late,
let the sunsets
arrive early,
let the evenings
extend themselves
while I lean into
the abyss of my being.

Let me lie in the cave
of my soul,
for too much light
blinds me,

steals the source
of revelation.

Let me seek solace
in the empty places
of winter's passage,
those vast dark nights
that never fail to shelter me.

—————————

JOYCE RUPP

Winter, a Season for Deepening

In the depth of your hopes and desires

lies your silent knowledge of the beyond;

and like seeds dreaming beneath the snow

your heart dreams of spring.

KAHLIL GIBRAN, *THE PROPHET*

The poetry of this season sometimes hides in the shadows. As the light and warmth decrease, and the dark cold days arrive, I sometimes wonder how I shall be nurtured until spring's return. I find myself dreaming of spring before I have embraced winter's gift. So now, in the season when we pull our cloaks more tightly around us, we ponder the gift of winter. I enjoy living in a geographical area where I can experience each of the four seasons. However, being a lover of the outdoors, winter cramps my style. A long winter's walk is invigorating, but the end of the walk finds me yearning for the warmth and comfort of indoors. Although I dearly love each of the seasons, I would have to say that winter is my fourth favorite. This should give you a little clue about my relationship with winter.

Although one of the spiritual invitations of winter, that of contemplation and reflective pondering, is high on my list of favorites, getting out in cold weather has always been something I dread. One of my first memories of winter and childhood is this: I was standing out in the snow, bundled up from head to toe in my snowsuit, woolen hood pulled down over my nose, hands imprisoned in mittens. I was crying (I

252

think it was more like screaming), "Let me out. Let me out. I'm locked in."

The challenge of winter is how to go within without feeling locked in. Winter has much to teach us about the inner journey. It suggests a time of resting and deepening, a time to gather the resources needed in other seasons. Winter has a lovely way of calling us home to what is essential. Among those essentials is the simple act of waiting in trust and not trying to make anything happen. We can't lock out all the cold, unpleasant parts of winter or of life. If we try to do that, we will also lock out some of the beauty. We can, however, learn to let some of our plans go, and practice receiving what just is. Winter, with its sensational kind of letting go, is a marvelous teacher and has secrets to share with us.

Let the land, the trees, and the plants teach you that what you see at first glance is not the whole truth. Winter's first glance speaks of barrenness and emptiness; yet that very emptiness houses a lovely truth. Listen to the emptiness. Listen for the truth. Perhaps it was in one of Thomas Merton's moments of contemplating this hallowed emptiness that he wrote, "Love winter when the plant says nothing." The tree or plant in exile from spring's sweet breathing appears to say nothing. On the other hand, there is never a time when the plant says nothing. It hasn't lost its voice just because it isn't flowering or greening. Perhaps it depends on who is looking at the plant. For those who know how to see with the eye of the soul and listen with the ear of the heart, even the barren plant speaks silent truths.

Let the plant rest. "*Love winter when the plant says nothing.*" Nothing, because nothing needs to be said. The plant is just being. It is simply living with the truth of itself as we all must learn to do. It is not thinking about spring when the green will return. It is not preaching eloquent sermons. It is not throwing color around. It is waiting in creative darkness. For those who understand this waiting to be prayer, we might call it a consecrated darkness.

John of the Cross understood well this mysterious winter prayer of going into the frightening beauty of the unknown:

> To come to the pleasure you have not
>
> you must go by a way in which you enjoy not.
>
> To come to the knowledge you have not
>
> you must go by a way in which you know not.
>
> To come to the possession you have not
>
> you must go by a way in which you possess not.
>
> To come to the way you are not
>
> you must go by a way in which you are not
>
> (*The Ascent*, Book 1, Chapter 13, #10).

The saints speak in holy riddles leading us into unexplored lands that seem barren at first sight. Winter is sometimes like that. Its frozen mask hides the vibrancy of life but reveals precious secrets about a mysterious hidden life. Only those who risk non-doing will learn those secrets. There will always be winter pilgrims who affirm life in the midst of darkness. All living things require hibernation at times. A little idleness is good for the soul of all creatures, both animate and inanimate.

Winter spirituality motivates us in our desire to touch that place within where we are wise beyond our years, that mysterious well-of-knowing so often hidden from our minds and hearts. We are called away from the traffic and the noise, away from our words and thoughts. We are called away from anything that would hinder our being. The way to that holy space within is the way of surrender. If we want to know God we must give up all our ideas about God and let the Holy One teach us from within. If we want to know God we must be willing to sit in the darkness, consumed by our longing. We will reach our well-of-knowing only when we have the courage to leap into the well-of-unknowing. There in that place of unknowing the soul is taught to trust. In that sacred space we learn to ask questions without needing answers. The question is part of the quest.

As we arrive at this dark winter time of the year, we turn our thoughts to positive aspects of darkness. We meditate on the fertile, unexplored, deep parts of our beings where so much creative energy, so much Christ-energy awaits us. The seed in the ground does not curse the darkness. Like this seed, until we surrender to the One who awaits us, we will not feel at home in the darkness. God is always waiting for us, longing for union with us. If we can become silent enough, perhaps, we will become aware of God awaiting us.

> This is where the union of wills begins—by becoming silent enough to risk experiencing the full weight of this inner touching of the heart and then to base one's entire life upon it. . . . One must step off the edge of the explainable, must risk believing in God, who like an eternal beggar, poorer than poor, waits to find the one who is willing to live for [God] alone. One must risk entering into the silence in which one is brought to say, "I am the one for whom God waits" (James Finley, *The Awakening Call*).

Each time you go into your temple to dwell, go as though it is the first time you have ever really prayed. When you do something for the first time, you may be excited, but also a little fearful. Let this be your winter-way of approaching

God. As you enter into that sacred space within, let this become your prayer:

> I am the one for whom God waits!
> I am awaiting the One who is awaiting me!
>
> Embrace the season of winter with hope. It is a good teacher. It will lead you to your inmost depths where God is contemplating you.

MACRINA WIEDERKEHR

Praying With the Gospel of Winter

....

U se the reflective exercises below for your winter prayer.

1. In her book *Growing Season*, Arlene Bernstein uses gardening to help her work through the grief of losing a child. In the passage below we see her thinning the winter lettuce she has planted.

> The lettuce seeds that I scattered in hastily prepared ground as a parting gesture before we left two weeks ago have all sprouted. They have made their first true leaves and are crowding each other as they continue to grow. They cannot all expand and mature in such suffocating closeness. Since I haven't yet turned the soil, I have no place to transplant them. Thinning is the only answer.

Reflect on any kind of *suffocating closeness* in your life that prevents you from maturity and growth. Is there anything that needs to be thinned out? What is too crowded? Winter is a good time to meditate on the things that need more space in our lives.

2. Read Mark 1:35. Follow the example of Jesus in going away alone to a place of solitude. This is a way of *thinning your lettuce*. Sometimes there are just too many thoughts, too many people, too much action. In the spaces between our words and actions we gain new insights into our living.

3. The sting of grief is often compared to the sting of winter. Many find a kinship in the season of grief and the season of winter. A season of grief, like winter, insists that you give yourself space for solitude. Reflect on this quote from Kahlil Gibran taken from *The Prophet*:

> And you would accept the seasons of your heart, even as you have always accepted the seasons that pass over your fields. And you would watch with serenity through the winters of your grief.

- Walk through some of your seasons of grief.

- What have these seasons taught you?

O Antiphons for Winter

O FROSTY SEASON,

Come! Come etch your face onto our windowpane.

Light a candle in our hearts each morning.

Reveal to us the beauty of waiting in the darkness.

Keep vigil with us in this nurturing season.

O Come!

O SEASON OF THE SHELTERED SEED,

Come! Come call us to be guardians of life.

Smile through the darkness of long nights.

Remind us that each seed needs a winter.

Invite us to trust what is shrouded in mystery.

O Come!

O SEASON OF THE LONG DARKNESS,

Come! Come with your misty grey cloak.

Cast your dark robe over all that needs sleep.

Surround us with faith in the unknown.

Protect us from too much light.

O Come!

O WISE SEASON OF REFLECTION,

Come! Come with your teachable moments.

Summon our spiritual powers.

Invoke our interior strength.

Heal our reluctance to wait for spring.

O Come!

O Season of Brilliant Sunsets,
Come! Come to all that has grown dim in us.
Sing your winter chants to our reluctant hearts.
Cast beauty into our winter world.
Reveal to us our own gift of being light in darkness.
O Come!

O Season of Mystery and Contemplation,
Come! Come into the fallow ground of our being.
Allure us from doing into non-doing.
Reveal to us the hidden wisdom in our souls.
Restore what is out of balance in our lives.
O Come!

O Wintry Storybook Season,
Come! Come lift memories out of the darkness.
Create new stories that have never been told.
Stir through the golden pages of our lives.
Recite poetry to us; tell us our names.
O Come!

O Season of Hidden Life,
Come! Come teach us humility.
Cut through the frozen ground of our being.
Soften that which has become hard and unfeeling.
Free all that resists the silent waiting.
O Come!

Winter Teaches Me

Winter teaches me patience:
Walk carefully on icy sidewalks.
Drive slower through snarled traffic.
Take more time to put on layers of clothes.
Wait for streets to be cleared of snow.
Be understanding about mail arriving late.

Winter strengthens my courage:
Go out into windy, freezing air.
Risk traveling on snowy roads.
Dress warmly and go for a walk.
Ski through woods, alone and free.
Be at peace in long days of darkness.

Winter brings me beauty:
Look up at the star-filled sky.
Pause to breathe the crisp air.
Vigil with steel-blue sunsets.
Marvel at frost etchings on windows.
Sink boots into soft, sensual powder.

Winter gives me silent hope:
Touch the terminal buds on branches.
Clear the snow and find green moss below.
Watch the sunlight fade, then linger longer.
Stand with the strength of evergreen trees.
Listen to birds cheeping at the feeder.

JOYCE RUPP

Courage Stones

....

A Winter Ritual

Small polished stones are loosely scattered around a candle on a small table.

Participants are invited to choose a stone (or let a stone choose them).

They return to their places and sit down.

Introduction

Describe some of the facets of stones:

Stones are sturdy, enduring providers of strength. Large rocks offer refuge as caves and give shade from the sun. Stones are used as firm foundations for buildings and boundary fences. Walls of stone enhance the beauty of gardens and parks. They often outline paths of labyrinths. Stones were a source for tools in ancient days and were used to build altars in biblical times. They have been used for good, but also for ill will and harm. Stone walls can be impenetrable, hostile barriers keeping others from their rightful places. Because of their strong nature, stones at times have been weapons that kill both the innocent, and condemned criminals. Stones of their own nature, however, are wonderful elements of faithful endurance.

That is why stones have been chosen as a symbol for the season of winter. It is during this harsh, cold season that endurance is especially needed. Stones stand strong and endure in all kinds of weather. Likewise, people with endurance stand strong in their winter season of life. They have courage to wait patiently in the silent fallowness of winter's empty months. They trust that they will have the strength they need to journey though the apparent bleakness and austerity of this season. They walk through winter's darkness with a firm belief that this space of life is a time of creative waiting, holding the nurturing energy that will one day birth within them.

Guided Meditation

Lead the group through a brief meditation on their stone.

Hold the stone in your hands.

These stones have had a home on our planet for billions of years. They have gone through immense transition. They have experienced dislocation and rough treatment by humans. They have lived through the various moods of Earth's constant changes. These stones have kept their unique consistency and beauty. They have continued to be resilient and enduring. Each stone has its own story to tell of strength and survival.

Use your external senses to "get to know" the stone.

Feel the stone with your fingers, notice smoothness, roughness, edges. . . .

Look at the color, variations in shade . . . its shape. . . . Smell it.

Feel its heaviness or lightness in your hand.

Get in touch with the mystery and secret of the stone, its personal history:

Consider how the stone was born from stardust, became part of the earth's formation from layers of compressed dust . . .

what it experienced of Earth's upheavals: earthquakes, glaciers, storms, rain . . .

how it spent much time in darkness, lost in the layers of the planet . . .

how it came to be here . . . where it was found, who polished it, who marketed it, and who brought it to this place . . .

how it has been treated . . . displaced, "beaten and polished" in order to have the shine and the smoothness it now has . . .

how it continues to be a sturdy, enduring element of life. . . .

Courage Stones

In her book *Kitchen Table Wisdom*, Dr. Rachel Naomi Remen tells the story of how she invites her patients to bring a small stone with them to the hospital the evening before surgery. She asks them to have caring family and friends gather around the bedside. They each tell a story of a time in their life when they needed courage, holding the stone as they relate this story of courage. Finally, the stone returns to the patient with the courage of each story left in the stone. Then Dr. Remen has the stone taped to the patient's palm or underside of the foot before he or she goes into surgery.

Your moments of courage may not seem like big ones to someone else. They might not be things like experiencing cancer or filing for divorce. Your story of courage may be the steps you take each day in trying to be kind to a family member, saying yes to getting well, offering forgiveness to someone who has treated you badly, standing up for what you believe, risking some new behavior, being a volunteer for a program that's new to you, or anything requiring an act of courage and strength from you.

Sit with the stone and reflect on a "courage moment" in your life.

(Allow some quiet time for this.)

Share the "courage moment" in small groups.

Blessing Each Other's Stones

Your stone will now journey around your group so that each person can bless it.

The stones are now passed to the left at the same time. Each person holds the stone they receive for a brief time. They "warm" the stone by wrapping both hands around it, silently placing a blessing of courage on it. Then they pass it on to the left, continuing this process until all the stones return back to their original place. Encourage the group to do this blessing silently and slowly.

Naming and Thanking Our Human Ancestors

Hold the blessed stone in your hand. Think of someone who has helped you to be courageous and resilient in one of your winter times.

After a brief time to recall who this person might be, each one in the circle speaks the ancestor's name.

Receiving the Courage
Stone's Blessings

Invite each one to hold the blessed stone to her head, heart, shoulders and hands. While this is being done, pray the following blessing.

(stone to head)   May you believe in your resiliency when you are wintered.

(stone to shoulder) May you have the strength you need to bear life's burdens.

(stone to heart)   May you trust the love and mystery within yourself to uphold you.

(stone in hands)   May your winter times of darkness become fruitful sources of growth, gifts to be given to your self and to our wounded world.

Clothed With Divinity

· ·

This ritual can be used as an introduction for reflecting on winter or as a closure after pondering the season. (If this is an opening ritual, you might want to read one of the selections on winter from Chapter Five.) Each participant will need a scarf, three feet or longer, or a shawl. Invite participants to use the scarf or shawl in the following ways:

Hold the scarf, or shawl, before your eyes.

Winter is a contemplative season of mystery. During our winter times we do not see clearly. Much is hidden from us. Remember what you seek, that for which you long, all that remains hidden from you. Make an intention to be more patient in living with the unknowns of your life.

Place the scarf, or shawl, on your shoulders.

Winter is a season of short daylight and long dark nights. Wintered spirits can be heavy-hearted and full of difficulties. Pray for that which weighs on you, that which causes you distress and concern. Trust that you will have strength to bear your trials and struggles.

Hold the scarf, or shawl, in your hands. Twirl it to the four corners of the cosmos.

In our own winter times we do not stand alone. Throughout our planet there are others who also know emptiness, waiting, loneliness, and seemingly unproductive times. Join with these people, creatures, and any part of creation that is struggling, or is in pain.

Hold the scarf, or shawl, up above your head.

Wintered earth holds the potential for growth: seeds snuggle in resting soil while terminal buds on branches wait for spring. Send encouragement to all persons, especially women, whose potential for fuller life is held under domination, all who are kept from knowing, believing in, and developing their innate talent and goodness.

Hold the scarf, or shawl, over your heart.

Earth slows down in winter. It is a quiet season. Turn your heart toward faith in the gift of growth that is within winter's silence. Enter into the season's restfulness. Pray for openness that you might grow from the wintry times in your life.

Place the scarf, or shawl, around you. (The leader now prays the following blessing for the group.)

> May this scarf remind us that we are clothed with divinity.
>
> As we wrap it around ourselves, may we trust in the Holy One's compassionate embrace.
>
> May the beauty of this scarf sing to our soul and call forth the hidden beauty within us.
>
> May the easy and fluid movement of this scarf lead us to seek ever greater freedom to be our truest self.

Repeat after leader:

> I am clothed with the radiant splendor of divinity.
>
> I am empowered to live the gifts I have been given.
>
> I am the beloved of God's own heart.
>
> I am embraced with unconditional love.

Now, clothed in dignity, aware of our inherent goodness, assured of our inner strength, let us enter into the wintered parts of our lives with deeper hope and greater assurance of the grace of this season.

Entering the Heart of Winter

Begin by relaxing. Let your spirit rest . . . gently let go of the busy things in your mind . . . allow your body to ease into peacefulness. . . . Take a deep breath and let it out slowly. . . . Do this three more times. . . . Gradually sink into a quiet place of calm and comfort. . . .

I invite you now to go within, to a quiet place inside yourself. . . . When you get there, place yourself in a lovely log cabin nestled in the woods. . . . It is wintertime, and intricately designed frost is on the windows. Burning wood crackles in the fireplace. . . . Feel the welcome warmth as you stand by the fire. . . . Turn and look around the room. See an old, comfortable looking rocking chair and move it close to one of the windows so you can look outside. . . .

Sit down in the chair and look out the space in the window that does not have frost on it. Outside there is a huge maple tree with sprawling, barren branches. . . . There is snow cradled in the crooks of the brown branches, and one bird with fluffed up feathers is sitting on a twig. . . .

The sun is partially hidden behind gray clouds. Now and then the clouds open and rays of sunshine beam through the windowpane upon you. . . . The sun is shimmering and sparkling on the snow. . . .

As you gaze out the window, you look more closely at the tree. Notice the small buds on the ends of the branches and twigs. . . . Each one is tightly closed. Look at how these terminal buds are filled out, pregnant with the new life stored inside of them. . . .

You close your eyes and imagine what it must be like to be one of those terminal buds. Let yourself become one of them. . . . Feel the winter air, cold and unyielding. . . . When snow falls, it feels gentle and soft . . . when pellets of rain drop from the clouds, you feel the piercing hardness of the ice. . . .

There are long nights. . . . In the freezing darkness, you gather the tiny wrappings around you as closely as possible, trusting that dawn will come. . . . As you wait, you sense within you the new life gestating. . . . Something within keeps moving ever so imperceptibly. It is strong and sturdy. . . .

You wait and wait in the darkness. . . . Finally the morning sun comes, but the intensity is not like it was in summer. . . . Something in you stretches toward light, longs for more warmth, wants to be alive and green. . . . Notice how every now and then the life inside moves slightly toward the light, stretching just a little tiny bit more. . . .

One day, you notice that the dawn is coming earlier . . . and the sun feels slightly warmer . . . the life inside of you stirs with more vigor. . . . You find yourself smiling, knowing that winter is now waning. You let your mind get a glimpse of green. . . . A little dance of joy skips around inside of you. . . .

Let your imagination leave the terminal bud and see yourself once again sitting in the rocking chair, looking out at the maple tree. . . . Remember the courageous terminal bud. . . . Remember the life within it. . . . Think about what awaits birthing inside of you, what waits in darkness and longs to be free, to grow. . . . (A long pause here.)

Take one more glance out the window into winter. Thank the tree and the terminal buds for their secret resilience and their hope. . . . Return slowly to this time and place.

Questions for individual reflection

1. What does your spirit most long for now?

2. Is there a part of you that is like a terminal bud, safely protected while it waits to stretch and grow?

3. Are there any situations or inner places that seem barren and empty in your life?

4. What do you find most difficult about your winter seasons?

5. Who or what is most helpful to get you through the challenging and disheartening times?

Integration

- Plant some flower or vegetable seeds in a pot. As you water and care for them, let your care be reflective of your belief in your own future growth.

- Go for a walk in the wintered land. Find a tree with terminal buds. Touch the buds. Hold them gently and listen to their message.

- Sit in darkness for ten minutes. Listen to the part of you that yearns to grow. Then light a candle. Sit in the light for ten minutes. Listen to your inner courage. Close by praying for trust and confidence in your future growth.

Carrying Winter in My Heart

This book provides a ritual for each season of the year based on the ancient custom of honoring the four directions of Earth. They use similar symbols to represent the directions, but the text of the prayers for each season is different. The prayers are focused on each particular season. The following ritual celebrates winter. You will need these symbols: feather, candle, cloth to cover the candle, an empty water pitcher, bowl of soil, and some seeds. Each of the prayers below can be prayed by various leaders or by the entire group.

East

Hold a feather. Silently place it down flat on the table or on the ground as a sign of the loss of vitality when in the winter time.

Great Spirit of the East,

my dreams grow dim and weak.

Songs of hope fly away like ghosts of long ago.

Enter my lost and wandering heart.

Greet me with your promise of new life

and your revitalizing energy.

Speak to me of blessings to come

while the hidden and the unknown

gestate in the dark spaces of my inner cave.

South

Hold an unlit candle with a cloth or cover over it.

Great Spirit of the South,

the sun hides from my bereft heart.

The light of consoling love has dimmed,

the warmth of self-satisfaction turned cold.

Soften the pain of my depleted spirit.

Surround me with the assurance of love.

Strengthen my trust as I stand in the shadows of life.

Let the remembrance of fruitful times gently hold me.

West

*Lift up an empty water pitcher to symbolize the emptiness of the
wintered heart.*

Great Spirit of the West,

the leaves of my good fortune wither

while the wind whispers the need to let go.

My good works fade and blow away.

I bend with vulnerability and weakness,

the basket of happiness emptied of its fruit,

the pitcher of love void of satisfaction.

Part of me fears the surrender required.

Empty me of what keeps me from growth.

Protect me from what leads to despair.

North

Place a bowl of dirt on a table. Push some seeds deep into the soil.

Great Spirit of the North,
my heart is frozen, my mind barren.
A glacial wilderness pervades my life
yet the seeds of hope are secretly planted.
They gestate and turn within me,
silent messengers of transformation.
I wait with faith-filled confidence,
hearing songs without a sound.
I will stand with full courage,
breathing deeply the ancestral air
which strengthens me.

A Celebration of
the Winter Solstice

....

Those present gather in a space that has as much physical darkness as possible. There is a cluster of candles in the center of a table which has cloths of navy, indigo, and other darker blues. The group is invited to sit in the silence of this dark space and listen to the reflection on winter. (You may wish to record the following reflective introduction so there will be no lights on during the reflection.)

Introduction

There is a tendency to want to hurry from autumn to spring, to avoid the long dark days that winter brings. Many people do not like constant days bereft of light and months filled with colder temperatures. They struggle with the bleakness of land and the emptiness of trees. Their eyes and hearts seek color. Their spirits tire of tasting the endless gray skies. There is great rejoicing in the thought that light and warmth will soon be filling more and more of each new day.

But winter darkness has a positive side to it. As we gather to celebrate the first turn from winter to spring, we are invited to recognize and honor the beauty in the often unwanted season of winter. Let us invite our hearts to be glad for the courage winter proclaims. Let us be grateful for the wisdom winter brings in teaching us about the need for withdrawal as an essential part of renewal. Let us also encourage our spirits as Earth prepares to come forth from this time of withdrawal into a season filled with light.

The winter solstice celebrates the return of hope to our land as our planet experiences the first slow turn toward greater daylight. Soon we will welcome the return of the sun and the coming of springtime. As we do so, let us remember and embrace the positive, enriching aspects of winter's darkness. Pause now to sit in silence in the darkness of this space. Let this space be a safe enclosure of creative gestation for you.

Song

"Come Home to the Darkness" (*Coming Home*, Kathy Sherman)

Sit in silence for several minutes.

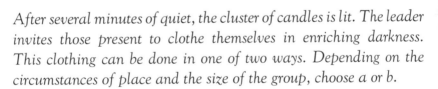

Reading

"Winter's Cloak" (see page 249)

Clothing Ourselves in Enriching Darkness

After several minutes of quiet, the cluster of candles is lit. The leader invites those present to clothe themselves in enriching darkness. This clothing can be done in one of two ways. Depending on the circumstances of place and the size of the group, choose a or b.

a) *Each one holds out her/his hands as a cup to receive the darkness that the leader names. They then clothe themselves with this positive darkness by moving their cupped hands a few inches away from the body, spreading out their hands, and proceeding to let the enriching darkness flow all around their body, mind, and spirit.*

b) *Have soft, lilting music playing in the background (flute, harp, or violin). As the leader calls out the name of the darkness, each participant moves with free form, receiving this particular type of darkness, clothing oneself in the type of darkness that has just been called out.*

 As the participants are performing the ritual, the leader slowly names the following kinds of darkness:

Kinds of Enriching Darkness

nurturing darkness

comforting darkness

sheltering darkness

restful darkness

restorative darkness

protective darkness

supporting darkness

love-making darkness

tender darkness

soft, gentle darkness

clarifying darkness

emancipating darkness

transforming darkness

First Dialogue

In dyads the participants now sit and respond to the following question:

Have you had a life moment when you have been positively influenced by darkness of some type? If so, what did you learn from this experience?

Guided Visualization

The leader now moves the group into a guided meditation on the winter solstice. Each one finds a comfortable position. (Refer to "Entering the Heart of Winter," page 268.)

Second Dialogue

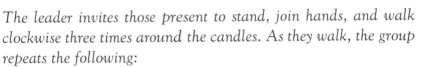

What kind of light does your spirit most long for at this time?

Celebrating the Return of Light

The leader invites those present to stand, join hands, and walk clockwise three times around the candles. As they walk, the group repeats the following:

We're coming out from the darkness of winter.

The light returns! The light returns!

A simple melody using these words could be created. All remain standing in the circle. The leader invites the group to name one hope she or he has for the future. After each hope is described, the group responds:

Wonderful Light! Return to our land and to our hearts!

Close with a chant or song that celebrates light and hope, or play lively music and invite the participants to dance freely.

Star Shining Ritual

And there, ahead of them, went the star

they had seen at its rising,

until it stopped over the place

where the child was.

MATTHEW 2:9

Introduction

The Christian season of Advent has as its central theme the coming of the Christ-Star into the world. It is a time to remember how God's Beloved came to restore harmony to a fractured world, to dispel whatever keeps love from shining through all beings. The Christ-Star, this Irresistible Love in us, this Radiant Goodness, is at the core of our souls. Advent reminds us that each of us has the light of this Shining Star within us. This special season assures us that we can radiate love and goodness to others.

Just as a star led the Magi to the Christ Child, so we are meant to be stars leading others to the Divine Love. Others are also stars for us, leading us to Divine Love. In each of us, the manifestation of Divine Love is a magnificent gift of hope and encouragement.

Uniting Our Star-Light With People of Our World

Each holds a lit candle. Stand and face the direction of East. Hold the candle in front of your heart to signify that you have Divine Love shining within you. Next, hold the candle out in front of you as far as possible, signifying an offering of this Love and Light to all people who dwell in the East.

As the candles are held out, those present name aloud the various groups of people who live in the East as a way of uniting with them. After this, all pray the following prayer, repeated after the leader.

Star of Love, shine your goodness through me.

Star of Love, unite my heart with the heart of the world.

Continue with this same pattern for each of the other three directions: south, west, and north. After all four directions have been tended, once more hold the candle to your heart and then move it slowly in a circle in front of you. Hold the light for family, friends, all loved ones, all who are a part of your circle of life. Send the light and love of the Star-Light within you to all who are in this personal circle of your life.

A Blessing of Star Shining

Sing the refrain to "We Three Kings" after each blessing is proclaimed by the leader.

Star of wonder, Star of night,

Star of royal beauty bright.

Westward leading, still proceeding,

Lead us to thy holy light.

May you often pause to remember that you carry a precious gift of Star-Light within you. *Sing refrain.*

May you greet this Star-Light within you with gratitude and amazement each day when you awaken. *Sing refrain.*

May you be led by this Star-Light to the places in your life that are greatly in need of love. *Sing refrain.*

May the Star-Light within you help you to find your way home to your heart when you have lost your way. *Sing refrain.*

May this Star-Light dance in your life and bring joy to those you meet each day. *Sing refrain.*

Closing

Star of Wonder, Radiant Goodness,

we turn to you as the Source of Love.

Keep us mindful of your transforming presence.

Shine this goodness and love on every person

with whom we come in contact each day.

Draw us to your irresistible love.

As we leave here we bring your love into our world.

May all those who suffer find solace in your loving Star-Light.

May all of creation be at peace.

Hold the candle in your hands again.

Walk slowly in a circle singing the refrain "Star of Wonder. . . ."

Conclude with all facing inward, holding the light out to one another.

ADDITIONAL RESOURCES

Arrien, Angeles. *The Fourfold Way: Walking the Paths of the Warrior, Teacher, Healer and Visionary.* San Francisco: HarperSanFrancisco, 1993.

Bernstein, Arlene. *Growing Season: A Healing Journey into the Heart of Nature.* Berkeley, CA: Wildcat Canyon Press, 1995.

Berry, Wendell. *A Timbered Choir.* Washington, DC: Counterpoint, 1998.

Conlon, James. *The Sacred Impulse: A Planetary Spirituality of Heart and Fire.* New York: Crossroad Publishing, 2000.

Dillard, Annie. *Pilgrim at Tinker Creek.* New York: Bantam Books, 1974.

Earth Charter. http//www.earthcharter.org

Guroian, Vigen. *Inheriting Paradise: Meditations on Gardening.* Grand Rapids, MI: Eerdmans, 1999.

Hamma, Robert. *Earth's Echo: Sacred Encounters With Nature.* Notre Dame, IN: Sorin Books, 2002.

Hinchman, Hannah. *A Trail Through Leaves: The Journal as a Path to Place.* New York: W.W. Norton & Company, 1999.

Horn, Gabriel. *The Book of Ceremonies: A Native Way of Honoring and Living the Sacred.* Novato, CA: New World Library, 2000.

Huber, Lynn W. *Revelations on the Road: a Pilgrim Journey.* Boulder, CO: WovenWord Press, 2003.

Kingsolver, Barbara. *Small Wonder.* New York: Harper Collins, 2002.

Matthews, John. *The Winter Solstice: The Sacred Traditions of Christmas.* Wheaton, IL: Quest Books, 1998.

McLuhan, T. C. *Cathedrals of the Spirit: The Message of Sacred Places.* New York: Harper Perennial 1996.

Norris, Gunilla. *Becoming Bread: Embracing the Spiritual in the Everyday.* Mahwah, NJ: Hidden Spring, 2003.

Oliver, Mary. *New and Selected Poem.* Boston, MA: Beacon Press, 1992.

———. *The Leaf and the Cloud.* New York: DaCapo Press, 2000.

Paulsen, Gary. *The Winter Room.* New York: Bantam Doubleday, 1989.

Roberts, Elizabeth and Elias Amidon, eds. *Earth Prayers from Around the World.* San Francisco: HarperSanFrancisco, 1991.

Rupp, Joyce. *The Cosmic Dance: An Invitation to Experience our Oneness.* Maryknoll: NY: Orbis Books, 2002

Schmidt, Gary and Susan Felch, eds. *Winter, A Spiritual Biography of the Season*. Woodstock, VT: Skylight Paths Publishing, 2003.

Shamir, Ilan. *The Poet Tree: The Wilderness I Am*. Fort Collins, CO: Better World Press, 1999.

Wiederkehr, Macrina. *Seasons of Your Heart: Prayers and Reflections*. San Francisco: HarperSanFrancisco, 1991.

Wood, Nancy. *Dancing Moons*. New York: Doubleday, 1995.

Whyte, David. *Where Many Rivers Meet*. Langley, WA: Many Rivers Press, 1990.

Music Sources

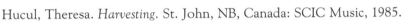

The Earth Dance Singers. *Earth Dance Celebrates Songs of the Sacred Wheel*. Sonoma, CA: The Earth Dance Foundation, n.d.

Frye, Velma. *Many Voiced Angel*. Tallahassee, FL: www.velmafrye.com, 2000.

———. *Music Spirit*. Tallahassee, FL: www.velmafrye.com 1995.

Fulmer, Colleen. *Dancing Sophia's Circle*. Albany, CA: Loretto Spirituality Network, n.d.

Haugen. Marty. *Gift of God*. Chicago: GIA Publications, Inc., 2001.

Howard, Juliana. *Heartpsalms of the World*. St. Cloud, MN: www.heartpsalmsoftheworld.com, 2004.

Hucul, Theresa. *Harvesting*. St. John, NB, Canada: SCIC Music, 1985.

Noll, Shaina. *Songs for the Inner Child*. Santa Fe, NM: Singing Heart Productions, 1992.

Novotka, Jan. *In The Name of All*. Scranton, PA: (570-347-2431), 2003.

———. *Melodies of the Universe*. Scranton, PA: (570-347-2431), 2003.

Reardon, Becky. *Follow the Motion* (a collection of original rounds celebrating the seasons . . . and the sacred diversity that makes the world go 'round.) Taos, NM: breardon@taosnet.com, n.d.

Rupp, Joyce. *I Open to You*. Notre Dame, IN: Ave Maria Press, 2004.

———. *Out of the Ordinary*. Notre Dame, IN: Ave Maria Press, 2000.

Sherman, Kathy. *Coming Home*. LaGrange, IL: Ministry of the Arts, 1994.

Vedder-Shults, Nancy & friends. *Chants for the Queen of Heaven*. Madison, WI: Mama's Minstrel Music, 1993.

MACRINA WIEDERKEHR   JOYCE RUPP

JOYCE RUPP is well known for her work as writer, spiritual "midwife," and retreat and conference speaker. A member of the Servite (Servants of Mary) community, she has led retreats throughout North America, as well as in Europe, Asia, Africa, and Australia. Joyce is the author of numerous books, including best-sellers *Rest Your Dreams on a Little Twig*, *The Cup of Our Life*, *May I Have This Dance*, and *Praying Our Goodbyes*. www.joycerupp.com

MACRINA WIEDERKEHR, O.S.B, is a Benedictine Sister at St. Scholastica Monastery in Fort Smith, Arkansas. She travels widely to offer retreats and conferences. Macrina is the author of five previous books: *A Tree Full of Angels*, *Seasons of Your Heart*, *The Song of the Seed*, *Gold in Your Memories*, and *Behold Your Life*. www.MacrinaWiederkehr.com

Artist MARY SOUTHARD is nationally known for her work as a visual artist, educator, and student of the Earth. A member of the sisters of St. Joseph of LaGrange, Illinois, she works in a variety of media—paint, plaster, paper, crayon, and clay—and is best known as creator of the Earth Calendar which has been a favorite in homes since 1979.